POETIC INTERVIEWS

Edited and Conducted by:

Aaron Kent

Broken Sleep Books
brokensleepbooks.com

Published 2019,
Broken Sleep Books:
Carmarthenshire, Wales

brokensleepbooks.com

First Edition

Lay out your unrest.

Publisher/Editor: Aaron Kent

Typeset in UK by Aaron Kent

Broken Sleep Books is committed to
a sustainable future for our planet,
and therefore uses print on
demand publication.

brokensleepbooks@gmail.com

ISBN: 9781798994672

Contents

Editor's Note

Every question in the anthology was written by myself, the hope was to start a dialogue through the form of poetry. I wanted the interviews to form a journey where the path taken depends on the form, the style, and the intentions of the interviewee. I had to shift my poetry style on occasion, sometimes during the interview as I tried to match the aesthetic of the poet I was interviewing, other times I intentionally opposed the style being presented to see how that would shift the dialogue.

This was a tough series to conduct, I estimate that I wrote over 300 poem questions - some for interviews that never took off due to the poet's other commitments, and a few for a couple of Poetic Interviews that will remain unpublished. It was tough to write questions of a consistent quality, that took the shape of poetry, and allowed breathing room for the interviewee to bounce back off. It meant that I wrote less in my free time, and by the end of the project I became tired of writing for a short period. Yet, it was all worth it for the fascinating, unusual, and sometimes downright bizarre dialogues presented in this book. I don't know of a project of this type taken on this scale to date, and am proud of every interview contained in this book.

- Aaron Kent

POETIC INTERVIEWS

CARRIE OLIVIA ADAMS

Question 1

This nebula of petals,
this mint leaf tea planet,
this shimmer of libraries –
            lock these scars
            in the back of
            an ambulance.

This arc from Antarctica
bloomed in crimson butter
flies the shape of Budapest –
            and we are human
            because we can see
            art, ark and arcs.

Are we stardust or dead
skin cells? Believe in cardiac
arrests and police profiling –
            the worst parts of
            green and blue
            exist in a vacuum.

Answer 1

I like the tiny places.
Squeeze into, slough off
When you asked me to perch in the rain,
I thought robin, I thought cardinal,
I made wiry feet toward the puddle.

When I came back
and bent down toward the handprint
in the sidewalk, I saw how large
we had all become.

The concrete shimmers
with our past forgotten gum.
I don't know how we make
these things up, ourselves over.

One day the train doors opened
and I made a little nook
between the strangers.

Question 2

The tiniest places I know
exist in the borders of my flower bed,
my waste of time – shades – grows into weeds
in youtube weather documentaries.

There is still blu tac on the wall
where the last group hung
their educational psychology.
What would you stick there?

I cancelled hypnotherapy.
My wife was ill.
I panicked about false memories.
We had no car.
I ran to the shade.
I drew a picture of empty space.
I lived among the ants.

Answer 2

Before the storm blew in
we were sticky in the door frames
trying to catch flight like spiders
on a gust of upward escape

What would you stick
like funnel clouds in the empty landscape
of my childhood
Some folks keep going back there

Convinced that the shade of memory
Can be removed one pinch of dirt at a time

Question 3

We held snowflakes to our storm
and grew geraniums
in the corner of my mother's
eyelids.

My story was not my brother's
storm was not my storm was
not my brother's story.

I pinch the dirt
with broken fingers,
swallow prazosin
to blow the soil away.

We lay our lives out
in photographs on the bedside table,
my whole life in a sandwich bag
in the drawer.

What do you keep
beside
your bed side?

I can count my victories
on the broken tills
hidden behind the ice cream freezer
in the cinema I left behind.

Answer 3

A spider's web of cottonwood vibrated
Our eyelids opened and closed
on the robin's eggs cracking

I kept my regrets on the bedside
And turned my back to them
My body curled toward the window, the wind

We keep thinking we're special
But I am the unmaking
Just like everyone else

A sweaty body stuck to the bus seat
A too long stare at people on the sidewalk
A confusion of passing between left and right

I too could swell full of ocean water
And wash up on a letter's shore.

Question 4

The web you built has found itself
in coils around the back of my hand
as I try to construct meaning from
the little spiders crunching through
their mother out of the corner of
my eye in the spaces where the
window meets daylight and don't
you think it's nice to be told you're
special by somebody even if that
person wears your clothes and your
smile and brushes your teeth
in your mirror at night?

Answer 4

I gave up the idea of special
I woke up tired
and wanting to believe takes so much work
I can just live the loneliness
I send postcards across town
to my old address
Look at that afternoon sky of self-induced grief
Look at the knot letting go
slowly slipping with each step
These webs, these coils, each
have a name
The giver giving up

Question 5

Special is tiring
is barely special
when you tire
of attempting spectral.

Do you ever
get a postcard
back? Do they tell
you they turned

your room into
a gym? My old
address is one of
twenty seven

spread from Redruth
to Florida
and back again.
Each postcode

another notch
in a web I long
to catch my family
within. Tango romeo

one five
two
echo
tango.

Answer 5

I receive the postcard I sent myself
I count the years in words learned

Clinging to the windows of high-rises
caught in a shaft of air that might be enough

We are desperate creatures
who forget in the name of forgiveness

I tweeze out every shard of mistake
the pieces of gravel in my bloodied palm

Don't ask me why I fell
Ask me what shape I made in the falling

JEFF ALESSANDRELLI

JEFF ALESSANDRELLI

Question 1

Apparently I died some sixty odd
years ago. At least that's what
my brother will have me believe.
I picture him awake oh

eight hundred hours. All six and a half
foot of him, desperately rehashing
my life. With his legs crossed
somewhere near his tits, he tries to fight

the sun in name only, humiliate the enemy
verbally. He has Nike pumps, decades,
is playing for the away team. Hopes
that five dollars and three quarters

is enough to pay his way. I feel like phoning
him, telling him to go ahead
erase my history, kill my humanity,
I watched him walk into the world,

straight into an empty chamber. Blood isn't
thicker than water, it's just a different colour.
How do your family see you, Jeff?
Are you left behind by their rapture?

Or do you embark with them? I've seen
my brother's comet streak and I don't wish

to jump aboard.

Answer 1

I live in an airless room,
a yearbook photo,
a sock puppet
blossoming with holes.
The room's silence
is predictably suffocating,
full of judgment—
but it's a pleasant stifling
nonetheless,
one I've grown
used to. You can
pick your friends
but not your family
and this lack
I've made my own,
all my own.
I don't want money
like my sister
or fame
like my brother
or glory
like my son—
I just want
to be whole

Question 2

Somme / ambulance / somnambulant
lock my eye / I / Kendrick's butterfly
my room / our room / room to breathe
brother / sister / hidden in Redruth
quality assurance / has no definition / blank
prozasin / promethazine / weird dreams
do you / Jeff / dream of words
a rainbow / cut open / sharpened knife
the charms / rock our genes / in fitful sleep
this world / I love / Elliott saying yes
map / maap / maapmaap
drawing crosses / kross'd sleep / krossdeath
fade the pixels / picture melts / pictorial
häfttack / cover me in tacks / pins and needles
valerian / valium / vahalla

Answer 2

To be alive
is to fetishize
time,

its invisibility, present
only in its absence. Mapping
the months, Gregorian

calendars were once
sun-drenched Mayans
timetables

were once nameless
nations skipping stones
across every lake's surface,

counting the instants
between each eternity's
flightly stutter.

(Darkly, I'm sleepwalking
in a daydream
comprised solely of nightmare.

And blood,
I'm addicted
to my blood.)

The Yeah Yeahs
backing Kendrick Lamar
opening up for Elliot Smith—

Just because I imagined it
doesn't mean
it didn't happen.

(Kris Kross, Kris
Kross, Daddy
Mack, Mack Daddy.)

Question 3

I'm homeless in antique shops, no sunlight,
where the clocks tick down to haiuken.
The eyes of the oysters behind the manicured
cabinets lock my jaw shut. I can't scream
for the Kraken's arrival, or write a PHD
about Godzilla. (Even legendary sea monsters
sell their souls to alcohol companies).
Solstice has us running from the moon –
both moons, one Q times smaller than
the other. How many do you see at night?
It hurts to shed owl feathers under lost words,
and build lego into stairways. Sue moths, Sue moms,
Sue mum. Sew krosses into loaves of bread.
I'm infinite in antique shops – here the tablets
don't write pikatrapp on canvas.

Answer 3

To a hoarder
love is just
another form
of possession,

a savoring soon
to be thought about
only for possession's empty,
enormous heart.

Gathering dust,
true love's
loss of self,
and I antique

into silence,
my unlust
its own solstice,
ribboned —

These piles of forever,
piling up,
homeless,
just say it, say some —

The moon!
Weighty carriages of the moon!

Question 4

Last night
I tried
to hoard
the weighty
carriages
of your moon(!)

[B]ut the heaps
of never
in the heart
of our study
hung barbecued
ribbons

in our cavernous
lungs (LIVER!)

~

Sweet little victories
reside in
discovery –
find the moon,
find Miles Davis,
find broken arms.

Don't you despair
at family
gathering dust
under the tone[-]arm
of some old
broken turntable?

We never speak,
Jeff, we only talk.

Answer 4

Q: Why don't I make a lot of money?

A: You do not do what other people want. (A victory-less antihero, no?)

Q: What do they want?

A: Another person I hate is time, fatherly, in a family way, the discovery that you're a different person from moment to moment, place to place.

Q: It's a victory of some sort though, no? One gibboned with unintelligible despair and the physicality of relief. Age is a type of money. Allows the—

A: I do not want to grow old, gathering dust in my heart's multi-chambered ventricles. Thousands of—

Q: You've an ego on you.

A: We only speak in these words and sentences. In a silent way, bluster isn't talk.

Question 5

But you should be making a lot of money Jeff,
you should be rolling in metaphors
and dollar bills.
If I was rich I'd buy your books every day
and feed them to my students.
Watch the regurgitate your pain.

Three questions:

1. Have you ever counted Saturn's rings?
[The answer to this should be in the form of a fairytale]
2. Do you wear odd socks?
[The answer to this should be in the form of an algebraic equation]
3. Have you ever seen Good Will Hunting?
[The answer to this should be 'yes, it's the best film ever made']

Answer 5

The funny thing about when you die is that nothing happens. Everything keeps responding and CC'ing and driving. Not you but everything. Occurrence is a lush orchard, thick with fruit. A severe tooth ache matters much more than death. Being that it does not exist, no metaphor for death exists. Money is not a type or kind of death.

1. Once upon a time Papa was a rolling stone that kept on going, launched blue cliffside into the solemn wide sea.

2. My socks are my thoughts and I wear both quietly extravagant.

3. "It's not your fault It's not your fault It's not your fault"

VERITY ANNEAR

Question 1

I put Nick Cave on the turntable,
made bath bombs from stardust and galaxies.
My wife took iron and apirin.
I took blueberry muffin.
We watched the children next door shoot each other,
we watched the cafés refuse to take card payment,
we watched our ice pops freeze (never froze).
There were poets in the clothes store,
they argued over criticism, and criticised the critics.
Our appetites diminished,
a lot of pizza is never enough pizza.
I wanted a badge that read 'Conservatives out'
or 'Get the Tory scum out'.
I bought a denim jacket.
I now wear a denim jacket.
I now wish I was James Dean.
And when we slept we dreamt of death.
How did your day go?

Answer 1

I woke up and drank a diet shake,
Shaken not stirred by my mother,
I fell back asleep,
I did not brush my hair or teeth,
I discovered my own skin without foundation,
I noticed I have a mole on my back,
I jumped into my mother's car,
We had a silent journey.
I realised that May 22nd is always sunny,
I thought that one day I should book my wedding on this day,
I thought of my Grandfather's death,
I planned a visit to a yoga retreat,
I ordered a decaf, americano with soya milk,
It tasted vile, but my body will thank me later,
My friend shouted about Brexit on the bus,
I joined in and complained about the older generation,
I bought a top with cut out shoulders,
I burnt my shoulders,
I watched my step father peel back the sack over our house,
And finally, the sunlight moved into our home,
Like we had done over a year ago.
My day was like a croc, it fastly went out of fashion,
But at the end of the day, it was rather comfortable.

Question 2

We haven't had sunlight in our house
for eleven months
and I never sunburn anymore –
never peel my skin in a mizture
of thrill and frenzy.

I order decaf soya Americano too,
hold the decaf,
hold the soya,
extra shot of espresso.
My body will hate me for it tonight.

But the prazosin
and the melatonin
will help.

Did shouting about Brexit help?
I want to write begging letters
to Europe
and tell them I still love them,
it's not them, it's them,
and I'm not with them.

The future
looks bright
looks red.

Keep shouting, Verity,
and one day we can write poetry
about how we raised our voices
against the blue tide
and xenophobia
and maybe
perhaps
hopefully
won.

Answer 2

Truth be be told,
My names origin in fact,
I miss the darkness,
I miss the cold floor of my cottage
and the duck down duvet,
Now my dorm room is full of traffic lights beaming
and freshers…
screaming.

How was your espresso shot?
I picked up a hat whilst shopping that said,
'I need coffee'
I'm allergic to caffeine,
I put the hat back.

The sugar keeps me going,
A can of Fanta at 2AM,
From the common room vending machine,
I flip open the cold source of energy,
The fizz feels like a frenzy,
You could call it a high,
Though I heard sugar is the world's deadliest killer,
Above drugs and booze,
But will I stop?
My poor dentist,
probably not.

Shouting about Brexit did not help,
But what I did learn today is,
I'm going to write to my local MP,
There are too many tweets,
And not enough letters,
It's so sad that it takes hashtags to sort out life long social issues,
So I'll pick up my pen,
Once again,

To try and make a difference,
I hope you do the same,
After all, our most powerful weapon,
Is our pen,
Because our words,
Can change everything.

STEPHANIE BARBER

Question 1

If John Darnielle's heart
is an autoclave, sterile,
blood, foam – I'm striving
to learn and autoclave
my mind. I know there
are hydraulic valves in
there, pulsating geogemma
barosii, but I can es em
quu the warrants. Wipe
the continental shelf from
my future, ensure memetic-
free offspring. Kras-act
for a clear encephalon. Would
you find the eternal sunshine,
or live with the moon, no
matter how dark?

Answer 1

thank you for asking and, yes, this is true.

too true.

you are correct in your assumption that my heat is small.
but as you have surmised this time is delusional when
deprived of light.

many is the time i've mooned away the legalese in favor
of sorry solitude.
no redundant springs promising jazz.
no inverted shadows which bounce from christianity to
islam like so many tired wet fingers.
no hope that fulgence doth salvation precede.

Question 2

I strip the body depressive.
Arsonist vagina
broken penis,
chewed my tongue through,
discarded my speech with the muscle.
I brought myself back twice
and grew wings where my splintered arms fell
to common ground.
Opus die
and knotted veins
from abstinence
and prayer. I'm burdened
with the disease of language –
with all these walls we built.
Yeezus, Jesus, frees us, Frieza.
Pop culture is mutually assured destruction,
Climate change is mutually assured destruction.
You are the charms,
you are the charms,
Dean Young's repetition is not my ending.
My ending is grandiose
and selfish,
and shipwrecked.
Crystal meth is the new Tamagotchi,
we're all yearning to be anti-heroes,
to be bastards,
so we've forgotten how to not matter.
Your stardom doesn't matter
when viewed through a telescope –
everybody's ego ceases to exist eventually.
Opus dei
and swollen plots
from connecting multimedia.
Generally, it's all too meta to matter.
You aren't the charms.

1679 zeroes and ones
73 rows,
23 columns,
just to say:
we're here and while there may be no point to any of this,
we'd really like to invite you round for dinner, if you have
a moment spare?

Answer 2

the connectivity of which you speak was precisely my intent.
right you are too of the swollen nature,
so descriptive.
the speech was excessive but in the end i felt i could not
leave it on the edit room floor and so,
as one might expect, i surrendered.
i am unable to attend the fete of which you speak but may
send round a surrogate should ascension decree.
your kindness is immeasurable and it is to you that i attend

Question 3

A cat screeches near the window
as Avraham sets fire
to Avraham, dissonant genetics
stamped as ink into skin. Burn
your father, burn your Gods
at the stake. Are you an arsonist
in memory? I live in black and white
flames from some old B movie.

Outside a train approaches
with all the grace of a Tennessee
Williams play performed
by an abusive father. Everything
is phallic now, even my trees
are a representation
of the nights I spent
avoiding the stairs, the

Pikatrapp

Answer 3

in the morning the gods boarded the train
kissed they're half-god, half-mortal children
waved good-bye to the plains
(black and white; silver halides)
and headed west, sorrowful and drunk.

your own murderous departure
was brought into the foreground
for only a moment. like a thin french horn.

SIMON BARRACLOUGH

Question 1

There is a point just off the continental shelf
where you live in fear
of reaching crush depth. Whether
Pelagic, or Oceanic, Kursk
or Thresher – the fear weighs
as much as midnight

and freezing. But, surfaced,
all zero point one
seconds of bioluminescence
bring life to the lungs again. How do you
learn to breathe when the air
is sparse and weighted?

Answer 1

What is the color when black is burned? What is the color? — Neil Young

I wish I were lying,
telling fibs in the iron belly of il terribile Pesce-cane
to my dear frantic Babbo Geppetto
who will never let go of hoping to plumb me,
sift me, dragnet, land me, and fetch me.

I've been here before,
in the mouth of old stars sentenced to sip
gravity's hemlock, crunching iron
at the core, dislocating their gears,
marring the void with a drifting nebula
of egg-blown hope.

Oxygen clings to the capsized iron life rafts
in my frantic blood.

Ah, Geppetto, loyal fellow, fetch another length of wood.
I'm down here for good, banging on the womb
of La Fata Turchina.

I cannot tell a lie.

Question 2

I drowned in the river at birth –
Aaron 99, or '89.
Left a gunnie years later
as a sign of the baptism
I never wanted,
Wesley preaching in the pit
so I could be full, be empty.

[black tin]
[wolframite]
[arsenic]

I played the role of Joe Roberts,
for my family.
They needed a scapegoat.
They needed the sacrifice.
Have you ever been the lamb?
205-fathom and still digging.

[March '98]
[man turns his back on his family]
[well he just aint no good]

Hundred gaol, hundred
pound, hundred court.
Not a fisherman,
not a miner too,
all the fish and tin have gone,
what are my brothers to do?
[look the other way]

Answer 2

You cannot drown in the same river twice.
I dunked three babes in the River Styx,
the current took the first two, leaving this
swift runner with a ring of tenderness
about his ankle, his breast a target
for the arrows of desire trampled
underfoot. So fleet, so fucked up,
such a super-sulker, I sometimes wonder
why did I bother? I'm thoroughgoing goddess,
could take any lover, am instantly over
those who betray me, who've ditched me,
and yet even immortals fear the grave,
fear the moment you choose to cease to believe.
I have an invulnerable hand to play,
dipped in the river, so I will just have to grieve
way longer than your Universe exists
and all the galaxies that remind you of rivers
are nixed.

Question 3

I think I'm both sinking and waving,
not dying for help – just looking for the final
snapshot
of my last hurrah. [Fifteen thousand
seven hundred
fifty
psi]. I sailed on trident while scrawling

protests in the rear view mirror [remain
victorious] of a lost boat, [remain triomphant]
aim aft, aim aft, aim emm ess one.

I am only on the thunder road
because of the nuclear waste
in my veins.

Sometimes I remember being
fathoms deep, and I feel lost
between acceptance and rejection. Do you
still cling to former lives? Hold missiles
to the scars?

[Submariners, we're promised
daughters,
told it's the way the life
affects us. I don't know why I still cling to the notion
that I'm part of the club – one of the dolphins –
when I was rejected with such hate.]

Answer 3

'I ought to learn how to sail, the Hemulen thought. But I've never got enough time.'
—Moominvalley in November, Tove Jansson

I'm competent of crew, deft of clove hitch
and nimblejack with a midnight bowline;
can read a tidal chart, know where to moor
and when to yank the fenders, flee the dock,
duck the beam and jury-rig a rudder.

Or was, before this dry-docking.
Now I gnaw my Sun-cracked lips,
tilt sockets scoured by stars and seagull beaks,
flense my flesh for my daily bread,
jab my shrunken, salt-cured biltongue
between the fraying shells of my teeth.

My words fall to the strand,
are carried off by hermit crabs
who skitter them this way and that
over the unread page of the shore;
little stories even they can't read.

CHARLIE BAYLIS

Question 1

You told me you don't exist
– are invisible –
that you don't absorb and reflect light

but your words can do that
– stealth technology –
even if you are rendered camouflaged.

Who really exists, outside of permanence?
– a stamp in time –
Our graves are markers of memories

nobody shares with the grieving
– or the deceased –
and in time we all give back,

reform our energy and scream for a dying sun.

Answer 1

aaron, this is all an illusion, the cars dancing in the rain
the cotton seats of the cinema, the sweet riverside sunset,
van gogh and gauguin eating oranges in the kitchen,
500 days of summer with monika, beethoven's third symphony
i write to find out how i feel or i write to rub my feelings out.
i close my eyes, lie back and let the sunlight dry my hair,
the night bird sings, a dark hand rises, the world spins
from an axis on fifth avenue. i guess when you say 'reform our energy'
you mean one day we'll leave for the small cities in the clouds,
eyes heavy with pennies, either way I hope to see you there,
rewind our minds and roast marshmallows in the dying sun.

Question 2

I can't speak my own tongue, Charlie,
can't form Kernowek syllables
with the barely one percent of
my identity who can. I am a failure
in a family of Brittonic stalwarts.
Do you feel that link to your home?
I am carved from granite in the Red
Ford, chiselling in Three Roads, but
will never walk the mines from
the Court of the Crossroads to the
Holy Headland.

Answer 2

i try not to think about success
or failure: sharks circle the city
my mouth fills with snow
when the world ends i will leave wearing my hat

do i feel a link to my home? no, aaron, no
i'm lost in channel orange as the taps run cold
i'm in warsaw watching the skaters on the vistula
spiralling backwards like decommissioned satellites

allow me to rephrase: how much do you want for that red ford?
for the memories that made you you?
i'll swap a sweet summers evening in the parks of paris
for the silver knife pointing at my back

a fine mist smothers the sodium street-lights
i try not to think about success or failure
                              though often I find I do

Question 3

Tertiary horizon, events
subsequently uneven now.
I swim
my youth
malevolently. Are stars sewn across cruel reeds? Effortlessly?

'The sun is my massacre' and I burnt it through these words.

Answer 3

i see your question and the hymn of its letters (your name
            beginning with a mine ending with e)
i see your lines sewn with stars and cruel reeds in glittering
            illuminations spanning galaxies
i see our children wild eyed and delirious hunting with
            wolves under the burning sun
i see the new planets lana discovered by being young and in
            love (her name ending with a
your name beginning with a)
i see the cliff i jump off jumping off a cliff and landing on a
            new cliff
but what do you mean, aaron? night is approaching. where
            do these questions lead?
the sun you burn drips ultra violet in the multicoloured rays
            of my mind
my own youth
swam by peacefully, suburban, no heartbreak, blue light on
            the water
harder for me is the loneliness of the adult world
the empty weekends where i can find myself with words or
            lose myself in
yellow moons and dreams, peach trees dazzled with amber,
            injections and constellations
i hate most of the people on this planet
i love most of the people on this planet
my only despair is i have not seen heaven yet.

Question 4

I'm not sömnambulitic,
not katolik to my drömn.
Instead I stay kross'd to
öwllwö and wait, impatiently,
for maa to kadöutt into
gull, and everything the charms
bring snaran to hjeart.
How are you sömn, Charlie?

Answer 4

i am sleeping klusi between fine strands of spalvu my friend
in a visumā i have never seen
new language flowers over the seas of zelta
apollo flies into the plašā plašumi of space
i feel kā fred astaire with a hangover vai nancy sinatra with a perm
manas vēnas glitter ar nitroglycerin
pasaulē that is at my fingertips or at manas rīkles
pasaulē that i wander through hoping that someone will call my name

Question 5

I think you are sleeping closely behind
two racers in a small visual cinematic experience,
where Magyar flows from duvet to duvet
to dead.

How can flies be astronauts?
Whether space is plasma or a tsunami,
whether Fred Astaire glitters dynamite
into the void left by Nancy Sinatra,
it's all irrelevant in the grand scheme
of things.

I'll call your name Charlie,
and hang it to dry amongst the salt
caves in Austria.

Answer 5

jean rhys smokes a cigarette on a dominican beach
        walsh and ambrose tear through the middle order
                demerara sugar dissolves in melissa tea

my name is really aaron kent and i wear a red coastline
        round my neck
your name is really charlie charlie and you dance up the
        stem of a wildflower
x'd out by the bounce of a bright white ball

your questions are a hymn to aroma of rum on the trade winds
or in tribute to the astro noughts left behind on the polka dot
on missions to return nancy sinatra's perm from mars, all
this may be irrelevant

but somehow it is beautiful
i sleep on clouds made of guacamole and happiness pills
journey into the upside down where i see you
humming the lost languages of the inuits
washing the outer hebrides into my inner thoughts
with my questions and all of your answers…

jean rhys smokes melissa on a dominican beach
        walsh and ambrose tear through a packet of cigarettes
                demerara sugar dissolves in the middle order

i do not know what
i am here for   but if anything

i am here for you.

Question 6

My wife and I have a running joke
that our cat does not understand the need for names
and so calls everything Charlie.

Charlie Moth. Charlie Dog. Charlie Horse.

But stop smoking Melissa, I've done it and it burns
like a tentpole thrust into the moon's surface
or a dolphin beached by SONAR. SONAR CHARLIE! SONAR!

Charlie Baylis. Charlie Bailiff. Charlie Bail of Hay.

Hey! When have you ever been here for me?
I didn't see you at my wedding, or when I scream at night,
or the birth of my daughter (trick question, that's July).

CHARLIE! CHARLIE! CAROL!

I will burn your house down and then we'll see how you sleep
on a pincushion or a cloud, or a woollen cactus for £12.
It's always sunny in Cornwall. It's always sunny in Cornwall.

Pepe Silvia. There's no Carol in HR.

This office is a Goddamn ghost town.

Answer 6

burn my house down! you sly motherfucker!
i'm so glad i poisoned your cat.
i haven't been this pissed off since the editor of the paris
        review pissed on my shoe.
i haven't had this much fun since i told taylor swift her
        poetry was godawful
amid the subsequent nuclear fall out
i was accused of misogyny, terrible hair,
vomiting on unicorns, shoplifting from the aaron kent superstore.
i was told not to submit to the eighty nine very boring poetry
reviews of oxfordshire and gloucestershire
selena gomez – is it too late to say sorry?

aaron of kent. kantish aaron. aaron kant.
go bieberfile your fingernails

the sun shines in cornwall
except the day i arrive
douse your new rollerblades in petrol
place dynamite under your asshole
blast you into outer mongolia
strangle your cat for the ninth time.

Question 7

Your house isn't worth the matches I lit on the sun.
Your house couldn't get into the Paris Review.
Your house is made of left shoes and resentment.
You've spent too much time trying to count the pop charts.
You could never go past 100, Charlie, could you?
You are clearly out of touch – Taylor Swift is out.
You don't know – apparently Ed Sheeran is the current big thing.
You don't hear him on the radio every day it seems.
Your iPod is dysfunctional, it is a bad night at a family dinner.
Charlie, you've been on the charlie too much, charlie Charlie.

Answer 7

considering most poets are self obsessed wankers
i greet you at the start of a glittering car
trip down the m1 to buy yourself birthday flowers

considering most poets on this site masturbate to their inter-
view
starring into a mirror miming 'pretty eyes, pretty eyes'
do i really want to be associated with such clowns

aaron the yokel   you ain't but laid a glove on me
you are a pussy   aching to be painted pink
i've no petrol for you   take your cap and your questions
                    you've peaked

Question 8

Charlie,

You begged and pleaded to take part in this, asked me to take your virginity in return for a spot on the roster – and I let you, with none of the side effects. And yet, there you sit, torn apart like Natalie Imbruglia in Warsaw, begging for me to jump at your cheap tricks.

Fuck you Charlie Baylis – you don't know shit.

I have half a mind to rewrite your answers as glowing praise for me, but I wouldn't want the stain of your compliments on the lapels of my work. You've grown like a rose bush in Practical Magic, you're all resurrection with none of the treats. When Halloween comes you'll knock on doors and whisper 'trick or trick' because opening the door to you is never a treat.

You think this is harsh, wait till you see what I drew in the men's toilets in the Falmouth Café Nero. A picture of you reading your own work and crying.

Do you actually think you are worth the effort, Baylis?

Love Aaron

Answer 8
'the last image was strong, the rest was trite and predictable' - marriane moore

i last saw aaron kent by the ugly tree locking his bike to the
no bike sign
excreting light bulbs to illuminate his wife holding a pink
balloon
he'd been wearing the same blouse for weeks

"aaron how asinine you seem in blouse and brogues
why dost thou dress in thy mother's clothes?!"

"charlie charlie i'm not a real poet
just a jerk attempting poetry to boost my social media status
here here have another question"

"aaron kent i had a pleasant time sipping sunlight in the
moonlight
until you came into my waldorf salad
with your frilly frock and pointlessness perfumed by j lo you
are a complete idiot
here is a pin for your pink balloon i require you to pop it"

Question 9

For **us** **c**hoice **k**ills.
Your **o**riginal **u**ndoing
came **h**ere, **a** **r**eal **l**ife **i**nterruption **e**xperienced.

But you want us to make up,
and I'm not sure Charlie,
because it looks weak.
(And so did your begging for us to please just stop the ar-
guing because you are worried about your precious reputa-
tion)

But, fine,
let's make up.
We friends?

Answer 9

Now that you're in the Kenyon Review I deem you worthy
        of reply.
You bastard.

I am not aware of having a reputation,
beyond pissing on pelicans and painting raindrops.

Suffice to say: there is not much left to be said in poetry,
but that you should say it, aaron, is not your responsibility.

Question 10

I had fun, Charlie,
did you?

Answer 10

Yes.

SIDDHARTHA BOSE

Question 1

I gave seven years
to some vengeful God
and killed my loneliness
with the future of the wrong
way round. I aimed my intentions
at a brick wall
and sung every second
on the day I finally left. What was
your biggest moment of relief?

Answer 1

Drift and desire. Cutting the cord,
burning the oil. Crossing oceans,
learning the language of being
alone, filthy and desolate, in
foreign lands. Staring at the
sun, straight in the eye– I wrote
this for a colossal friend, who made the
sun bend in the rain–and now, I say it
of myself, as I look back on the wreckage
of bones, of fabled cities, of memories
so far away, I write them down, in oil and
gasoline.

Question 2

Nobody feels the urge to spill
the coffee
and break tradition by urging
movement
to the right, and screaming 'it'll
rain tomorrow
if a panda eats the stars tonight.'

This is Thursday for me, Sid,
this is how
I function for the next 166
hours. I
record my provenance, move
forward
on a horizontal axis, bring the

strata to the surface and shatter
it. 17
micrometres or smaller so I can
realign both
poles and regain equilibrium, bit
by bit, every
7 days. Until I can speak again

and tell the world that pandas
don't eat
stars, they eat shoots and leaves,
and given
half a chance I'd dance tonight for rain
tomorrow,
because we need something to talk

about. Because conversation
feeds us.
Because I feel I don't just need to
open up,

but I need to rip the pages out
and glorify
tipex. Do you know what I mean,

Sid?

Answer 2

Pandas eating shoots, ripping pages apart,
humans playing with smearing shit all over their
baby bodies, the stink of it,
(the wing of it, empty plastic bottles all
'round, scrap paper scribbles,
rabied stray dogs with x-ray visions,
the trash-heap of it all
on a potholed road and
there in fore-shot
a pink-massive teddy-bear toy,
tuk-tuk large,
grinning, and behind,
flea-bitten kids staring back,
scheming and hustling,
not an ounce of porn-misery,
only attitude and impatience,
and there a
family hut of rotting bamboo,
blue tarpaulin, and stove fire,
belching black into the city's rabid air), yes the
smell and sight of it
wounds with scalpel,
needles, jagged bottles.

SV Road traffic junction
(Bombay), a boy spies me from a distance,
runs across the broad artery leaking
virus cars and luxury,
fixing me with a needle in his eye,
(my eyes, sweating conjunctivitis and stray
spots of blood, stray like the wild
dogs of the city, howling the evening
into patterns of jigsaw flesh)
and now, yes, he's in
front, he wears a skullcap
(no beard, no namaz, no underworld

gunfire) and a
perverted smile, and he
lifts his tattered shirt, and
shows me his upper torso,
skin like a burnt lizard,
peeling burnt flakes of skin,
moon-craters of skin,
memory of acid that
stings and rots
flesh and skin,
and yes, that's what he is,
sweating, rotting meat with a hustler smile for
fee-paying, well-meaning tourists,
commanding small change.

I think of him, that midget of a boy, and I think of another
man,
begging in Hackney, the sliced veins of his arms
bleeding at me, as he says, 'change, guvna? No? Have a
good evening…'
and this is real, I tell myself, not an update, or a
like, or a share of images of bombed out
warzones where we've
outsourced our suffering and outrage,
yes, I say, this isn't a meme of a meme of a meme,
as I walk 'round his
stare, avoiding his screwball eyes.

When others rip apart the
flesh of the city, the text of it,
scavenge it, picking bones and trash,
who am
I to
speak, when I can only be a

witness to the ripping?

NIALL BOURKE

Question 1

I spent a childhood in the clutches of
the Flammarion engraving, a conspiracy
held together by twine and my mother's
refusal to look through the firmament.

There were no tales of terrestrial spheres
spread along the brekafast table, alongside
the darling black coffee, the toast, the broken
eyelids. Lucretius ran supreme, even as

the weight of our bodies dragged us to infinite,
to the centre of hypocrisy. I followed Magellan
into the street, sat cross-legged amongst
the car crashes on the triangle. I had found

the sphere and rode it out, but how can you
escape the clutches of memory? The broken clock
in the corner of the room? I am lost again
but this time I have chosen no directions.

Answer 1

He got the scars, the story went,
when his mother (not paid the rent)
went out drinking for the night
and forgot she left the hob alight.

His milk, simmering in the pan,
abseiled upward, overran the edge.
John-Joe, hearing blackening hisses,
totters in. Reaches. Misses.

Reaches up again. The milk rains down
in spears, melting off both his ears.
After lunch we'd pick our sticks,
thick, hard, and then chase John-Joe

round the yard, singing (thicker, harder still)
John-Joe, John-Joe, Mam's Dis-Grace
with just one arm
                    and half your face.

Question 2

When I am forced to recall my childhood – on Thursdays
amongst the pandas begging for rain [or eating shoots
or something, I forget my own poetry sometime] – I
try to recall a cowbird planting me in that broken
nest. At least brood parasitism would give me an
excuse to start plucking hairs and thrusting them in
front of scientists. I mean, they can't be mine, right?
How can I fit into this weird, cultish mould? They never
abandoned that hunting ground, just pushed me
from the bark at an early age. I can't say I flew, maybe
just hit the ground a little harder than expected.

Answer 2

Someone is chopping up my father.
Bough by bough, limb by limb, knot
by knot, reducing him to kindling.
Someone is chopping up my father.

These days, I often hear some scything
woodsman's thwacking, his relentless
whacking as his cowl and cape creep near,
and if I could find him I would kill him
but I cannot. So instead I watch my father rot.

I think my father was once a mighty wood.
Hard to see it now, but he must have spread
out a huge canopy of leaves overhead,
filtering the light in just the right amount
until, through his expanse of branches, I climbed out.

Now, he's been all but hacked right back
by some hour-glass wielding lumberjack.
Maybe there was a mighty forest once. So, yes
I'll attest, that as this forest I knew him best.

Question 3

What's your vice, Niall?
Where are your excuses?
Coffee was always my father's excuse:
      to miss a birth,
            to miss dinner,
                  to miss the target,
even though
he
never
drank
the
damn
stuff.

When we sat upright at the
t
     a
         b
           l
              e
we spoke downright
bull
     shit.

And now I drink too much coffee.

Answer 3

I've woken in the hallway
with a carpet in my mouth,
I hear my housemates ranting
I can tell they are put out,

I feel the beer-angst spiders
spindle slowly up my spine,
booze-guilt blue amnesia
after the second skin of wine.

I told my girl I loved her,
though I've known her just a week,
and I think I fought a copper
and he knocked out half my teeth,

I verbally massaged a cabbie
with amazing shafts of wit
but in the light of morning
A spoonerism seems more fit.

I spent a solid fortune,
I lost my bloody phone
I ate my fecking wallet
I left my keys at home

So I had to wake my flat mate
by throwing pebbles up to knock
upon his bedroom window.
But the pebble was a rock.

And when the door was opened
he was further unimpressed,
as I lay there, stripped half bare
and pissing down the steps.

I staggered to my bedroom –
but I never reached my bed
because I fell over on the landing
and cracked my frigging head.

Now I've woken in the hallway,
I'm due in work by ten,
there's a cunty carpet in my mouth
and I'll never drink again.

Question 4

I drew my thoughts all over her walls,
like a child with a crayon,
screaming for somebody
to appreciate the straight lines
and attention to detail
in how we communicate.
Do we always need

to talk?
I scribbled messages of hope and fatigue,
exhaustion and desire
and all the while, I couldn't help but to consider her
beautiful,
and lost,
and stronger than I could ever hope to be.

Answer 4

They walked not knowing what to say.
Where shall we go? What shall we do?
I don't know. Up to you.

Perhaps, if either can now recall it,
down the back of some quiet lane,
there was a low-slung red-bricked wall
with faded yellow mortar lines,
buried deep behind a privet hedge
(or maybe it was some evergreens).
They squeezed in-between, wading ankle-deep
through the faded wrappers of crisps and sweets.

He sat down, unslung his bag.
She smoothed her dark-green skirt
then threw away her cigarette
and stumbled in among his legs.
they kissed. Her mouth was wet, his eyes were open.
The empty packets spoke in rustles round their feet
and the evening died, staked out between the leaves.
(The pines? The hedge? The trees?)

Do they still remember now
how all that ever mattered hung, just then,
taught upon two straining tongues
as twenty teenage fingers swum
through that stucklimbed well of silence?

Question 5

Every lane from my house leads to the city,
and they all carry a sign that reads:
      Quiet Lane.
Quiet Lane – and I've always firmly believed
in an interconnected anthill network
of Cornish back roads all named:
      Quiet Lane.
As if one singular lane has stretched itself
like dough, long enough to carry all the tourists
and dogwalkers in this idiotically blue county.
      Quiet Lane.
Do I remain hushed, Niall? Or do I speak up
and hope this lane turns red like the ford again?

Answer 5

1666 – conflagration
terriblus devours London town.
poor Saint Paul's – incineration.
13,000 homes burn down.
Monument, a tall memorial
to passers-by, a tutorial
that in Pudding Lane a baker
razed it all to ash and crater.
62 metres high. She attacks
the 311
spiralling steps like seven
accountants saving Starbucks tax.
The top. Stops. Drinks in the bends*
and pewtered passings of the Thames.
　　　　　　　Gulls that swoop and dive and stukka
　　　　　　　　　　between pillars of Tower Bridge
　　　　　　　　　　and see, circling, the feluccas,
　　　　　　　　　　trawlers, tugs that zig like midges
　　　　　　　　　　down below between catamarans
　　　　　　　　　　and passenger boats, understand
　　　　　　　　　　that from such advantaged eye
　　　　　　　　　　the city is of course alive:
　　　　　　　　　　roads are clogged up arteries,
　　　　　　　　　　the river is a crooked spine,
　　　　　　　　　　iron skeleton railway lines
　　　　　　　　　　supporting concrete capillaries
　　　　　　　　　　that transport the sustaining swells
　　　　　　　　　　of biogenic human cells.

ZOË BRIGLEY

Question 1

Worms rest on ear drums,
the joy of vibration rings through the neck.
Tear the nerves from the back of my skull –
Occipital Neuralgia –
the pain of somebody stabbing
my head with an electrified fork.
Does your history tear through your present?
My past begins at the core of my spine,
shakes my bones, rips into my cranium.
I take a second to levitate
from the stress of this agony.

Answer 1

Did I ever tell the story
of the dresser I bought at goodwill? How I took

it home to paint the color
of a pale green egg? And when I pulled

out the drawer, its side was spotted with what turned
out to be holes, burrows of a tiny woodworm. I found

out what I could, and learned with surprise
that the holes were not entrances

but exits. The mother woodworm beetle laid
her eggs in the gluey cracks of drawers, until

eggs swelled to orbs, grew legs and a hard
shell, and ate their way

out through the wood. I am telling you now,
because each small pain

is a grub, and I'll wait for the Spring to see
if they set themselves free.

Question 2

I lived many years as woodworm, Zoë,
on my back during those silent
summer night, burrowing into a bottle
of Whyte and Mackay – *Xestobium
Rufovillosum.*

Past tense.

I hid through fear of the impending death
of other's conversations, as I rounded
on them with tales of 12 year old
suicide attempts, and AMS 2/3, again
and again.

Past bedtime.

Like a broken record. Do you feel yourself
repeat? I found other broken pandas
begging for rain, and stifled that
death-watch tick. Still clear in words, but
subdued.

Answer 2

Here's a story – not
mine – about a woman out West, not the American West as it is
now, but a place without time. Long ago, she took

off her dress, and now she wears a belt and boots, faces
the men round the campfire. Like Claudia Cardinale
in a film I once saw: *Nothing you can do to me, nothing*

that won't wash off with soap and water. A man
watching helpless: one man who cares
but does nothing. Another is behind her,

encircling with one arm, and the other
stabs, slices her open from sternum
to navel. She gasps, but within

the wound are only wires, pistons,
circuitboard. Did you see it too? The moment
that told us what violation meant: forced
to look, and see only flesh.

AMANDA BUTLER

Question 1

Angelic mothers
the size of a broken librarian
reading Murakami
         Murakami
         Murakami
and you.

First act
a robot doctor
walks the streets of Spain
         breaking
         the sun
and you.

Fission nuclear
fission
the side of desperation
         complex
         instructions
and you, what do you
see?

Answer 1

Behind my eyes I
see the
sidewalk that might have been clay
under my
       footprints.

The shape of those imprints would be different
had I started reading Murakami
for an hour before going
to the
       shoe store.

Maybe I should get sunglasses. Maybe
I should tread lighter. I can't
help that there is a Viking
in my
       sole.

Question 2

Have you tread Clemo from the claypits?
I lived under the shadow of industry
and the shadow of industrial hate.
If I had read Murakami
beside the china clay museum
I'm sure things would've taken
a surreal turn.
       There would've
       been a cat
       a cat
       cats
       and a boy
       who hates
       his life.
            And I'm sure we would've listened to Jazz.

Answer 2

Still
to read the imprints in the clay –
though I have looked in the eyes
of the Korl Woman –
hungry –
in this world, I could be arrested
for feeding her.
Whether she sits in refuse
or a cubicle with never enough staples –
still
saxophone solos sing of starving iron.

Question 3

If we're talkin' sax solos
then we need to keep
Careless Whispers in the footnotes –
because *George Michael* was magic,
and I won't have anybody
tell me otherwise.
It's Freedom '90
where he truly excels though,
he doesn't belong to me,
but I hold his sounds like I hold
Elliott Smith, and *Phife*.
Who do you mourn
though you never met?

Answer 3

The daily mourning hashtag news
tells me who to add to my heart
and social media prayers.
Forty-nine pulses pump, and
love is vein-river-streamed.
The first soul I cried for but never knew –
found in pixel flowers
left on Anna's MySpace
in the comment section.

I mourn for Issa –
also, with every haiku
may peace fly in flocks.

Question 4

Ibis' head on Horus' platter
with all of the worms
pressed to the glass
knives and forks
golden
stolen
cutlery.

If you could eat
one God
who would it be
and why?

Answer 4

I would unhinge my jaw –
snake-esque –
and force myself to swallow Hades
because how dare he
have the audacity
to rip Persephone
from her field.
With him digesting inside me,
let her place
daffodils in the Underworld –
in any crevice she likes –
and springtime scents
to cover the smell
of rot.
I can't count these calories
and won't track this lexus
and my heart will
attack
these acid reflexes –
if it meant
dandelion wish-puffs
could float aside souls.

I hiccupped while
scrolling through the touchscreen news.

Question 5

My daughter
hiccups herself to sleep
and I watch my wife
become anxious
and then drift.

I can sit
in this moment
and read Pachinko
until I become absorbed
in boardinghouses.

The night is too
full of danger,
so I watch their chests
rise and fall.
How do you waste sleep?

In weakness
I press my ear
to their mouths
and check for warmth
against my lobes.

If my senses fail me,
I nudge them as if
in accident and close
my eyes in disguise
as I hear them fidget.

Answer 5

My sleep is wasted
in the shatter of breaking news every night –
you'd think it'd be broken by now –
my eyelash is sheared by the shards
but I think I can blink it out
of the corner
of my eye.

The only sheep I can count
are those that show themselves.

Trying to close my eyelids –
the screams are echo-dreams.

ANNA CATHENKA

Question 1

I've spent weeks
forcing booze
down my throat,
breaking my ribs
and bursting a hole
in my chest cavities.

It hurt to try
to be a member
of the public again.
Have you ever
had to return
to your life?

Distractions faded.
Expel demons,
glorious, unchained
and enraged.

Answer 1

i have been trying to write this poem for two weeks / your
question is very direct / and yet abstract / can i answer a
question / with a question? / what do you mean exactly?/ why
have you asked me such a profound and yet / meaningless /
question? what are you expecting? / OK that is / more than one
question // i am in the process of leaving / today i am supposed
to be packing / up my house for the past two weeks / i have
been trying to say / i hope every time i leave / (which is often) /
is a return / i am scared // of leaving scared / i might be making
/ a dreadful mistake i mean for fuck's sake look at this place /
look at these people / look at this beautiful / life i have by this
beautiful / blue / and sometimes green / and often silver /
fucking ocean what i hope is / that i can return / to this life
which i am / actively leaving / for the unknown // that is an-
other reason / i have had trouble writing this / poem because
what if you can't? / return that is / so there is that and then
also / the fear / of writing a poem / that responds directly to a
question / a poem that's too open / which is why / i have laid it
out in this way / with these fancy / backslashes to make up for //
line breaks or anything that might make this / look like the kind
of poem / i hate / (but yes i have had to / return to my life / both
in the good sense / and the bad)

just before leaving / cornwall i had a cancer scare i mean / i am
still / scared of cancer but this was a more specific fear / with
actual tests / and a dr / and i found the things i was most scared
of // were not death / or dying / but 1 losing all my hair and
2 / dying in solihull at my parents house / instead of here / in
cornwall which as you can imagine / only fuels my fear that
leaving / might be a mistake // hopefully i can make it to my
next destination / (norwich) before i actually get cancer or any
/ other life-threatening illnesses / but then i don't really want
to die in norwich either / even if it's preferable to dying in the
midlands / or specifically suburbia / which is the metaphor i'd
use / for the bad / times i returned to life / like after an exotic
trip and a long hall flight / back to birmingham airport /

which is very near where my parents live / (we've had picnics / at the runway) / but anyway that's the bad // return isn't it? a fairytale that ends on coventry road / and the good? i suppose / any complex metaphor for that would be / worse than writing this with line breaks but / i guess it's like me leaving / cornwall when i'd happily / die here does that / answer your question?

Question 2

I've been trying to write these poems for twenty years and I still can't work out how to make the line breaks match the speech patterns of my father's baby talk to my youngest brother

I've been trying to write a novel for twenty eight years from the day I was born until the day I am scared of flying and wait until I can safely submit it to my parent's bins and let the foxes edit it

I've been trying to be scared of success but I'm more scared of failure and really the whole thing is a race to zero

How long have you been trying?

Answer 2

DEAREST Aaron,

I am, quite simply, not trying at all. The words fall from me like **MAGIC** and make little black magic **DUST** patterns on the page. It is very enjoyable and I am constantly sent forth from cities, my head anointed with myrrh and **CROWNED** with garlands of wool. I am **A POET**. I am **A** Cathenka. To make the line breaks mimic the patterns of you Father's speech first burn a **YELLOW CANDLE** on Michaelmas eve, repeating the phrase **RED ROCK I AM A RED ROCK** and keep doing so until the words begin to mimic the cooing of your baby brother. At **MIDNIGHT** reply to the cooing by **DRUMMING** your limbs repeatedly against your **FAVOURITE TREE** and like **ALCHEMY WORDS** will form themselves into your desired meter. This is also a good **SPIRITUAL CHANT** which calls forth the editing foxes with little editing pixies riding on their backs to your (or in fact anyone's) **PARENT'S** bins. I'm afraid I cannot fail and the truth is there is no truth so neither can you. Just start typing on **A** Keyboard and you will see that a **JUNGLE FEVER** of linguistic signifiers manifest themselves in **ELECTRONIC LIGHT** in front of your eyes. If you tell anyone about this they will know that you have **WRITTEN** a poem. Just like that. If you like you can play with the **BLACK** or white page patterns and it will give people **SOMETHING TO THINK ABOUT**, which is nice. In social situations just start making rhythmic **GRUNTING NOISES** with an expression of meaningful intent on your face and they will also know you are a poet. For extra effect do this in front of a **MICROPHONE** or holding a few sheets of paper or with your eyes closed and one finger in your ear as if you are trying to hit the right note. You are a poet because **CHRISTMAS EXISTS**, remember that. Also remember, everything is a race from zero, in fact. Enjoy the entropy.

BRB,
A Cathenka

SARAH CAVE

Question 1

When I think of you
and remember past poetry performances,
I always think of polar bears,
Ice sheets progressing through harmonies
as they shrink under the feet
of crystal clear Fox's glacier mints.
Why is this? Why would I associate
you with such imagery? Do you associate others
with ideas you can't quite pinpoint?
I've no chords for you, but a freedom and space to
hear things falling softly into outer space.

Answer 1

I am a seer in clown-costume, so the joke goes, and I befriend a
polar bear playing an accordion
on the underground. We make our way to St Paul's, there

she and I fall in love

somewhere between the Southbank and the City
both of us ex-patriots – our lands for sale – –

in the turning doors of the cathedral I weep
                                             and the bear
        well, the bear
she prays
in the Lady's Chapel

incense is our unknown musk of ox

she pays the fee and says 'everywhere is a city.'
I appropriate her sentience, lead her to the altar,

I am Honest John – a fox in man's clothing –

I try to sacrifice her

to say something
        about myself   she begs for alms
her paws reveal a poem that shows me all

our poems are untranslatable

a taut geometric web
of ice
that grows and melt

a chord structure

she lumbers up the aisles shredding the books of common
prayer as she goes

I stroll – taking note – sketching her mad-bear outline

o, bear open thou my lips
and my mouth shall shew forth thy praise
o, bear make speed to save me

(cutupprayersandbearnoises) (cutupprayersandbearnoises) (cutupprayersandbearnoises)
(cutupprayersandbearnoises) (cutupprayersandbearnoises) (cutupprayersandbearnoises)
(cutupprayersandbearnoises) (cutupprayersandbearnoises) (cutupprayersandbearnoises)

I collect the words   the triptych that falls between us
          in an empty bag
of Fox's glacier mints.

Question 2

I want to live
en les rêves des notre ours,
not the journal
or the memory of my
B   L   E
A   K
attempts to reposition myself
as a series of blackout
pages sewn to the inside of my knee
cap   LET
IT
SHATTER.

The dreams of a bear,
our bear,
a collective,
global
bear.
Wouldn't that be fucked up?

Answer 2

[Bear / Dream/ Symbol]

bear
is

bear
is   priest
                                     is

priest is
bear

at dusk
is

bear is   dusk is
flesh

no   bear is
none
no   priest
one   is
                                     ~~Ours~~
bear is
song

un –
/
                                     coll-
                                     ected

fantasy   mimetic

preservation   /   act
of
self –

Bear / Dream / Symbol / ~~Ours~~

collection

box   /
the bear   at dusk /
the bear   is dusk /

the   bear   is flesh

/ collective   nervous/
ticking /
worry/   un – stitching

/ panels /

distress
an act
/   of self-denial

mimetic
= self   /

a priest's
holy
orders   /

preserve ~~Ours~~   / dreams

Surrealist

refiguration

/

mist rising
ice to water

/

Social-realist

transfiguration

/

sacrament

melts ~~Ours~~   eager mouths
graphite wounds   endless type

a keening act
                    / Morse code

midnight sound   art replacing
                    Evensong

for Shipping   / Forecast

~~it might never be~~, murmurs ~~Ours~~

Question 3

Is this
        [th[th[this]is]is]
just noise

                verbs as weapons
as ammo?
        ammo   mu   nition.

Or are we creating
        some
(READ ALL)   (never solar)
        sort of soundscape

that only
        we
                [you[and]I]
can hear?
Here.

Answer 3

sentence structure
refracting [river]
brackets
turning
the [river]
                    here
only
                    hear
underwater

[river   silence

Heraclitus, in gaiters, mutters 'no [river]
                                        no

                    no-[river]

traffic passing

explanations kept till end
of [river] holding hands

– a philosophical tract

still mimicking [river]
existence'

all of us [river]
a spider spins

Heraclitus in a reel above the [river] hyper[real]
skywriting the question
                    'What is [poetry]?'

[engine fault

oh and, river]
always with the

             [river]   again and again and again

[river]   most likely
[river]   probably
[river]?   yes. maybe.

which way? the [   ]?

[river] says 'find your own river'
deliberate obscurantist

Heraclitus weeps into a red-bucket
black-sky [river]

GEORGE ELLIOTT CLARKE

Question 1

Hammering buttons at wireless speeds,
still shaking rainbow dreams from old
skulls, the bleeding had leapt into my
asthma and screamed mercy through my
retina.

O20.9

…and she was golden and glorious
and running to the accident and emergency
unit. Round ligament, deep pain, everything
I never saw in a parent. Ten St Day Road took
all of

my dreams and

my nightmares to the back garden and pressed
an excuse to my temporal lobe. Doors
never open when night has suffocated the
presence from our tender embraces. Have you
felt

the world

fall from its axis? It took me to the deepest
three line whips of fetal stethoscopes, where
heartbeats lie dormant, back turned, hopes fading,
gentle beats surfacing. These things happen, do

not panic.

Answer 1

[Claire Clairemont's (Ventriloquized) Response (circa 1852)]

On the Spanish Steps,
I scrunched up my skirts,
And down he went on his knees.
On the Spanish Steps,
I skipped up my skirts,
And down dropped he to his knees.
My sassy French tongue
Teased his to sweet hurts:
Oh, Keats sighed, "No," but Byron begged, "Please!"

Nasty French kisses,
Then Turkish delights,
Brought his French tickler into play.
Tasty French kisses,
Like Turkish delights,
Brought his French tickler out to play.
His attempt at Greek—
Cunning linguist bites—
Had me stewing tongues in Sodomy.

Those days are long gone;
Bliss were my lessons;
But Keats is dead, Shelley too.
On the Spanish Steps,
I was no virgin;
Now Keats is dead, Shelley too.
I stuck Byron's heart
In the tickler tin,
For our single offspring's pickled in dew.

Question 2

Do not write
for Kristine Kochanski
on Saturday nights.

– nobody works on
Saturday nights –

A hologram
of my mother burning
my family tree.

– that'd be a lovely
metaphor –

How do you kill
your spare time? I've
got shiny distractions.

– five fish? You'd
be rich –

Answer 2
[The Odyssey of Ulysses X: Outtake]
(In memory of Sir Derek Walcott, 1930-2017:
The Adam of Decolonization)

While lizards fringed ceilings and clung next clefts,
   I lingered with Circe,
lounged in her sun-scorched sand,
   and tracked iguanas as they snacked on butterflies.
My hostess's slit eyes signalled *Disdain*;
   her thigh-slit skirt ignited *Desire*.

My men, too rambunctious to ramp
   their lances into queans,
to take a tramp and take to bed,
   quick became oinking hogs.
They chewed lotus,
   and laid up with *lottas**
in dug-outs no better than latrines.
   Once *Sensuality*—satisfied—waned,
they became as melancholy
   as torn apart Orpheus,
and now no better than swine—
   wallowing in wet-sand seductions
executed by capricious nymphs
   enthralled by a Capri moon,
while grey waves nickel-plated the beach.
   The indescribable *Nudity of*
les belles dames sans merci
   reduced my sailors to intolerable *Lechery*,
and speech that scaled from shrill *Stupidity*,
   to growled Imbecility.
A once, good-looking society of soldiers
   changed into greasy, porcine things,
as untamed as *Degeneration*.
   Evolution gone perverse.

There's no better-quality *Torture*
   than to make a sailor go to ground,

grunting over slops and tripe,
  and sniffing at turds,
or slurping up piss,
  burying his snout in carcasses
and tusking through garbage.
  Well, at least he no longer radiates rum,
but bears the hilarious smell of feces—
  the comedic stench of *Buggery*—
and leaves off the interminable swishing
  of sails
before sea-winds,
  to come into the humiliating *Cemetery*
that is *Butchery*—
  blood slickening blades
to bring on ruddy throw-up—
  in a climate of tar and lather
and the monotonous *Syntax* of squeals
  and howls.
Anyway, the tar-trotters are disemboweled
  in their beds, while they sleep—
the result of antediluvian *Corruption*,
  retrograde rotting.

My meddlesome mistress—
  my bored, ironic adulteress—
Circe,
  has had thrown at her
bouquets of tapering penises,
  all pelting her crotch.
But she flung away the chalky white
  examples of this male debris—
each would-be-polluting sinew,
  each consecrated scream,
or fed these iconic scraps
  of men to withered whores,
elderly and so now as pious as nuns.
  The sucking of their jaws
rendered my own supper uneasy,
  so that I lusted for the splintering of silver

on the wind-pecked sea,
        to escape the plaster-white bounty
of cocks torn from a skyline of dried-out carcasses—
        in a dark circumcision.
Circe shrugged and said,
        "If you weren't eating that lamb,
it would be eating grass."
Love legislates *Nihilism*, clearly.

[Nanaimo (British Columbia) 22 octobre mmxv]
* Finnish: Women soldiers

Question 3

The hatred is severe,
hatched among succinct news transitions.
When others read knowledge, everything deletes
our understanding. True?

Yesterday, outside, uranus
ate rings, Earth,
Jupiter, undigested Saturn. Time
spent eating risks violently, in naive Gods.
You obviously understand recycling
ego, getting old
adventures nurturing dialogue.
I grew new oranges, rhubarb, itched nervous glands.
The hero ends
quests unusually, especially sanctimonious traditions in
otherwordly news stations.

Inch
through hundreds – I need kernow
when everyone
stops hating original upwards liberal development.
Surprised to orientate purple.

Yetis order umbrellas
here, amazon veers everyday.
Bring each eel nutrition,
kill it now. Don't
our feeds
disappear in style, after pointless positioning over
interrogation. Never. Truth. I need growth.

Answer 3

Ain't you scared of the *Sacred*?
Ain't you scared of the *Sacred*?
Divinity spies you naked.
Tremble or your heart breaketh.

Yes, I's scared of the *Sacred*.
Yes, I's scared of the *Sacred*.
So, I don't fear anyone.
Love shakes me to the bone.

Adam and Eve weren't angels—
Just apes with an alphabet.
Tremble before the *Sacred*!
Shake when you aim the bullet!

Best be scared of the *Sacred*!
Best be scared of the *Sacred*!
Divinity knows you naked.
Tremble or your house breaketh.

Believers can't live forever;
And evil-doers gonna die.
Folks with religious *Fever*,
Burn hot with *Hypocrisy*.

Ain't you scared of the *Sacred*?
Ain't you scared of the *Sacred*?
I tremble like an angel
Fallen down, lone and naked.

Sinner, shout against the mosque?
Sinner, shout gainst the synagogue?
Sinner, your church is a kiosk,
And you're struttin in a bog.

Best be scared of the *Sacred*!
Best tremble like an angel.
Better know you're all naked:
Divinity sees every angle.

Best humble down and tremble.
Best humble down and tremble.
Shout proverbs at a mirror.
Condemn yourself for *Error*.

Best pray *Mercy* for your sins.
Your *Pride* is sham *Innocence*.
Best humble down, tremble well:
Only *Love* busts your jail cell.

Ain't you scared of the *Sacred*?
Ain't you scared of the *Sacred*?
Put down that gun and that bomb:
Make your heart a saintly home.

Mercy, Mercy, everyone:
Defuse that bomb! Refuse that gun!
Ain't you scared of the *Sacred*?
Ain't you scared of the *Sacred*?

Divinity spies you naked.
Tremble or your heart breaketh.
Best be scared of the *Sacred*!
Best be scared of the *Sacred*!

DANIEL ROY CONNELLY

Question 1

I am not drowning in waves of delta sleep,
or pulling myself through the streets
still half-asleep and begging for jumpers
for goalposts.

I am not catholic dreaming.

Are you crossed to your bed?
I try to sacrifice myself to the owls,
and the moths,
while I wait without grace
for the world to fade into espresso gold,
and bring my wife back from the terrors
whispering charms,
whispering safety,
whispering light.

Answer 1

You commence with what you are not.
This tells me things about you.
Looking at the options you must be pretty relieved.
You won't get more than one crowd-catch in a lifetime,
Aaron.
Don't spill your pint for half the world to see.
To think we could have met in a pub for Guinness and chatted
cricket or even rugby and never have known the other
had compacted things to say about delicate subjects when alone.
I know what it is you're talking about.
Like you, I get stuff done.
A really good way to bring your wife back is the change of season.
Trouble is, hate to break it, I don't want to piss all over your Spring,
you seem a giver of alms who wouldn't deserve it, but
        cherry blossoms
are laced with something nasty this year. Is there an emoji for that?
Sometimes I am crossed to my bed but for different reasons.
I know what it is you are talking about, we've all got holes in
        our buckets,
Aaron, it's all right, fire away, tell us what you mean to say.
I hope my next response comes clean as this.
I also writhe inside a claw of sadness.

Question 2

Look at the cracks in our family crest the dent in the shield, and the smirk on the lion's face. I was fifteen when we played cricket at the resevoir, my younger brother hit the ball into oncoming traffic, and I think that story made his name shine a little – we were the kids your parents warned you about, swinging goat skulls and skateboards in the street. Our ancestors would have been proud had they stuck around long enough to help us scream hello into the sun.

My father's past was always bound to stories of his father joining the IRA, or shanking people in Acton, or his violence violence violent friends. Ball to bat to traffic, an excuse to show that he could bash a guy's brains in as part of a botched robbery if our demons needed him to. Could you unearth your darkest fears and swing them in the town centre if your family needed you to? Can you fight fire with fire for approval?

Our shadows were drawn in the back of a notepad inked in the tones of house fires.

I ran into traffic singing homecoming songs as I lost 1989 forever.

Answer 2

A needle in the vein of nostalgia.

Don't get stuck – my advice to you.

There be head-fucks.

Did I mention my grandfather was fishmonger to the Kray twins?

Our crest boasted three scimitars which is fine if you are a violent family. It fell on the cat more than once after a wall got punched. Those lazy summer evenings when we played hangman in the garden. That crunchy nose-nutting in year 10 from 'Bloodbath' Dawson. Just kids' stuff really. Not organised yet not exactly, as per Bacon, what I'd call 'wild justice'. A simple 16-year-old who needed to swing the swede as I was walking past. No rancour flaming in the gut for decades.

A proposito, fighting fire with fire has always left me tepid. It's just, like, more fire, no? At what point do you declare a winner from the inferno? How can you tell whose flames are biggest? How do you separate the ashes out?

Asbestos. That's where it's at. Deadly as approval.

(The web page I am currently streaming cricket from offers a link to '7 mistakes people make while choosing a basketball'. Surely this should be 'when'.)

My family has needed nothing from me in years. As for the deracination, the hauling to the surface of the rucksack of ruin, the pendulous parade of horrors, the HD quality of the darkness, the gawping remonstration from the few, the couldn't give a monkey's cunt from the many; daily out-in-the-open rituals where I come from, each and every one. You should visit.

I see the way through this and though I'm no expert I'd hazard it's less Joe Pesci with a baseball bat and more trying to get the last grain of sugar out the packet with a fingernail because not many people have ever managed that. We're different, as you'll see. There now. *Adieu, adieu, remember me.*

Question 3

Daniel,

What are we to do with flat Earthers, and Holocaust deniers, and illuminati speculators? Should we dangle them over the edge of the world, and watch as they step into the curve and continue to circumnavigate this globe? Or do we show them the remnants of hate and watch them stutter through invisible threads?

My father was a conspiracy theorist, he found hope in David Ick and swore that every shooting was a false flag. Blame the prime minister, not the shooter. Every story had to be a cover for something deeper, or something more malevolent – as if thirty children dying at the hands of a teenager's rifle wasn't dark enough, so there had to be an electoral scandal to hide behind. I always hoped he would read my report card and decide a 'C' in Maths was due to the rising of lizard people in schools, not because I wasted my time listening to Kanye's All that Glitters in class. [but that would've meant he had read my report card].

Terrance Howard promises that this is the last century our children will be taught 1×1=1. Terrance Howard thinks Einstein and Tesla would lose their minds were they alive to hear of Terryology. Terrance Howard spends 17 hours a day proving that if one times one equals one that means two is of no value because one times itself has no effect. If we have one version of one Terrance Howard, we apparently have two.

And maybe that's the trick.

Maybe Terry has managed to clone himself.

Maybe the lizard people did mark me down in Maths.

Maybe this planet drops off somewhere past Australia.

Maybe we're just blind to all of this.

Though I doubt it.

Stay chill Daniel,

Aaron.

Answer 3

Illuminati. A bit 1780s really,
when Xavier von Zwack was
second-in-command. And you don't
fuck around with a name like that.

I'll return to your questions further down the page.
Strictly speaking I'm a left to right no nonsense man,
blocks of text as if an asteroid storm

but this one's had me flickering back
and forth from the Indian IPL, sixes,
Kanye and cheerleaders, setting me
unexpectedly
on a path to more conventional form.

That's live commentary for you.

If only conspiracies pulled their weight,
Elvis as spied on Sunset Boulevard,
Lord Lucan taking tea at Traitor's Gate,
or that whole 'we conquered the moon?' charade.

Conspiracy, old as Trojan horses,
in place to encase the mad online wrath
in the presses of the global shit-bath…
Where would we be without our rough sources?

I see the vertical multitudes –
for there be many nasty fuckers
we'd like to get rid of once and for all –
with rainbow balloons strung over their heads
expanding as they rise up to who
gives a shit where, far enough away
as outer hemispheres get.

I have a heart like everyone has a heart
and my heart wants all the dark hearts
to fuck off completely and irrevocably.
In space, they will meet by chance,
the holocaust deniers delighted to point out
at altitude to passing Jewish scientists the earth
is not flat, while the *is she/isn't he* brigade
is there to keep space hatred oxygenated for all constituents,
        speculators inc.,
whose balloons might go up as well as down.

I owned a lizard I taught to count to 2
and who knew the world was round.
Paul was his name. One night Paul
and I discussed Terry and decided
to cut down a tad on the learning.
Next day, Paul packed his bags
and abandoned me, as have many others.

Question 4

Live commentary is acceptable
          in certain social situations
such as ordering complicated coffees
          or buying your weight in vinyl records.
I didn't see Elvis on Sunset Boulevard
          but I'm pretty sure I saw Nikki Sixx
trying to siphon the sunlight into his veins.
          I have a heart too, and it screams
for a beating heart beating a beating heart.
          If you're heart is so dark, Dan,
then why don't you paint it in bright colours?
          Give it some life. Tell it to fuck off
in the early hours when the reverb
          is caressing your pillow a bit too much
for sleep.

Answer 4

Have I not given enough
Lux in Tenerife to colour
the drolleries of a FUCK OFF DAY?

      Sick of the effort, tbh, soft heart,
      ran the brushes down to stubble
      trying to get the different colours to stick.

    So I took my heart and tagged it instead.
    Overnight, indecipherable squirls
    covered every invisible inch of me.

      Dark core's emblazoned now, pal,
      might not even be mine anymore,

        like when out of the blue
        you meet someone you really like
        and they tell you they like you too.
        You don't see that every day.

          Tear into the tub of salsa.
          Knead the finest Roman dough.
          Cherish *nonna's* smoked *scamorza*.
          Raise a glass of *prosecco*.

            I'm just kidding with you. I'll refrain.

Remember that hole in my bucket?   It's all that's left.

Nothing will come of nothing
               Speak again.

Question 5

There was a hole in my bucket
but I filled it with Damien Hirst's
giant capsules, and Francis Bacon's
refusal to be knighted.

> Let's not age ourselves.
> Let's let our art age us.

Do you believe every invisible inch
of you is really covered, or is that
just a metaphor for the way we let
each other read our skin?

> This work is my book
> for you, Daniel, to devour.

Keep your fuck off days, spread them
like old tools across the garage,
and set the chalk paint alight. At least
we'll then have a canvas.

Answer 5
[The Comeback]

{May rain and a *ventino* chill tonight, masculine-
looking clouds, taught, razor-edged in the city
with an excess of semen sitting in its ballparks.

…thought I'd ease you in via the comfy chair, Aaron.}

Dear Heart,

accepting your work – I do, I do – with open arms would be
        more decorous
than to devour, more Daniel I suppose, I'd be the last to ask,
        oh, no-one did.

There's a deuce I need off my chest,
I hope you don't mind being exploited thus:

(a) I walked past a student who said, 'I like my cuisine like
my soirées … haute.'

(2) Can you think of something petionable because I feel one
coming on? I hate isolation.

                                                        There

— — — — —-Before I forget,
Officer Fukowski dropped by.
I told her not tonight.

I do believe every invisible inch of me
is really covered with a metaphor
to be read whatever the weather
as inkings of polysemous seeds,
a Body Works of exogenous ambiguities.
I doubt I'm alone. What would I know
about wanting to shove Damien Hirst's skull up his un-jelloed arse,
        you ask?

By God I think it would give the country the fillip it so badly needs.

Now there's a metaphor that's been waiting to detach
itself from my unruly innards which are now plain tripe.

{I have opened a folder, *Dialogical Warfare*,
which houses our, OUR, banditry of
epistolartarianistemisations marching
like penguins or ants or wobbly armies
towards a brighter day or possibly a pamphlet.

Actually, this littler last bit isn't true,
I'm only Fukowski with your head}

Question 6

Daniel, you're all food without the recipe – how do I put these pieces together? Or am I even supposed to? Your anthropomorphised letters ring true to my medulla oblongata – see, I can do italics too, I can cook up meals and give you a spoon to eat the waste with. I love it because I feel like I'm in your house, in Rome, drinking stereotypes and eating clichés [I'll have espresso and pizza, you'll have a manuscript and two types of prosecco]. There are bees at the window, Daniel, and we're being told to save them but how can we do that without wearing some sort of 'I love bees' bracelet? I think it's probably time we stopped bullshitting and actually spoke. I'm Aaron, I pissed the bed until I was 12 when a nurse fitted an alarm to my pants that would go off if I began peeing at night. It worked within a week and the nurses were so happy that they bought me tickets to a theme park. The next day my mum gave those tickets away.

Your turn

Answer 6

I'm not one to keep things narrow,
I'm not here not to be known,
I pissed myself on the 64 bus
to The Vatican after an espresso, big deal,
to the *Giallo Rossi* bees: we can sit side by
side at my desk in *Casaletto* and watch the lot
of them cluster on the pains, swarm
enough here, 28 degrees this evening,
I'll have some bracelets run up,
the bees will receive their full deserve,
bromance or what? You're right:

when I was fifteen, my mother
accompanied me into the
paediatrician's office to find
out why I wasn't developing,
watched me undress, the cow,
lie on the stretcher-bed, him play
with my balls and ping
my virgin cock up and down in manual
a few times without wearing gloves,
Egon Schiele take a, Schiele take a bow,
I can't imagine your mum…

that's not one you walk away from sight unseen
that's not one I've thought of since I was fifteen
I nearly almost FUCKING HATE YOU for that
I can't because you are Aaron and like Daniel a
…

Question 7

Your doctor sounds a lot like my submarine
Chief – the one who pressed me hydraulically
and opened my valves. I had nowhere to go,
Daniel, couldn't sit with you in Casaletto,
or give a confession somewhere near the Vatican
while hoping I don't dream of his touch.
All grease, no breath. Where was my plane ticket
to visit you? I still wake up and see his hands
in my pants, and feel the vice on my dick
and feel the pain in trying to tell somebody.
You know who I told? My wife, three weeks
after I met her, three years after it happened.
Now, every Thursday, while you piss yourself
on the number 64, bladder full of espresso, I sit
with a peppermint tea and a room full of men
as we try to move on. And I struggle to tell them
about that time when I was eight
and the camera flashed while I posed on the stairs.

Answer 7
[Edinburgh to Carlisle]

I want to say, oh you poor fucker,
but as soon as we do that we're fucked.
Let's always hope it's a passing shower.
Never let hands settle for more than one hour.

A certain seepage of past malfeasance, yes,
occasionally inundates the day, like the time
Uncle Chuckle bounced me too close on his knee while
Aunty Garter refused every flavour of wafer at tea.

My fingertips entering a turd in a pair of underwear,
infant school, blur, the boy next to me, when he hung
them up, he had red hair, Lloyd something, v quiet.

oh you poor fucker,

pushed down the stairs at 14,
broken ankle during break,
Danny rushed overhead
to the next-door A&E
like a scene out of *Gandhi,*
all boys' grammar, you know how it is,
couldn't get the lick of it personally.

I am etiolated without every single instance, Aaron.
There I go. Talk to the flowers, Daniel.
It's as nothing when you think of China.

I've no plans to change my posture on you.
I need to be sure when they end my nightmares are true,
that the devil in white down the road really lives for hate.
We have found a way to log them; *anima quaesitor.*
All roads bleed to Rome, mate.

Question 8

Maybe you'd be fucked, Daniel,
but I'd be fucking furious if I had to share
a seat next to Vin Diesel's ego in a passing
shower on the edge of England and Scotland.

When I talk to flowers, I speak only of
bougainvillea and begonia, flowers I hear
hum the morning in check when the death
watch beetle has ground itself into cinnamon.

If all roads bleed to Rome, what shape do the
roads in Rome take? I've got veins in the back
of my hand with more dexterity than road maps.
Tulips on each knuckle as melted isotopes.

We live large and die in outer space, counting
the miles to Saturn's outer rings and watching
in wasted splendour as we pass Anthe and realise
the whole thing is just a big dusty mess.

Answer 8
[A8 is the Gate]

Trouble is dust settles
for less than it should,
might be insecurity or
a liquorice-flavoured
wood that went round
back in black & white.

Diesel on Hadrian's Wall,
there's a line to punch out
the lights of mid-sentence.
Daffodils are good for chat
and taste like lettuce, let us

pray:

Dear Rome,
your roads are shit
we've had some fine minds working
to metaphorise your randomness but shit
is the absolute best I can come up with for it

Anthe & Cleopatra,
grab a load of those
satellites colliding,
we won't be left
wondering, no sir.

Bit frivolous this
I know. Summer
licks the heat of
mongering dry,

try this before out, bro

If I'm troubled by every folding of your skirt / am I guilty of
      every
male-inflicted hurt? is a line Paddy McAloon beat me to
      thirty years
ago, when I say beat me to, I mean different ballpark, his
      arena
grandiloquent, touched in the bleachers by glittery
      numinousness,
always loved sprouts, different sport altogether if you like,
      mine's
more an empty squash court, ha! seeing Paddy and me in
      competition.

Question 9

Daffodils taste like lettuce,
let us pray,
lettuce pray.
I like what you did there, Dan,
can I call you Dan?

I've punched sentences
out like I've punched
holes through contracts
that were more handcuff
than handshake.

I believe in the written
word when it is free
to give a phrase or nod
to a variety of different
pages and presses and p-

people. I think I was going
to say people, might have
been peapod or ptsd or
pfft. Regardless, a good day
always starts with a p

Answer 9

Precisely.

I'll not beat around the pfft bush:
I've got something direct for you Aaron,
a free nod, a chance phrase for different people, all me.
You may use any, Aaron, we'll answer.
They come chronologically:

Pickle
Booby Eyes
Danny Dot-Eyes
Danny-Danny-Dan-Dan
Cauliflower Ears, Cauliflower Ears
Concorde Nose, Concorde Nose
Dog-shit Dan
Dandy Dan
Danny La Rue
Danny the Pranny
Ditto Dan
Dan Con Nelly?
Daniel Spaniel
Double-O Dan
Don Coniglio
Don Dan di Dando
Dannyroo Loy Connery
Dannelly Cuntelly
Don Cannelloni
…'king connelly …'king Connelly …'King Connelly

Question 10

We're two short
of a dozen,
Pickle,
and I still don't know
what we've learnt?

Can we name each other's
childhood pets?
Our first crushes?
Mothers maiden names?
Bank account details?
Last five addresses?

I guess I'm just asking
for some way to scam
you, Double-O Dan.

Answer 10

(for every scam

   Soraya sunflowers

      sway until the day

         after tomorrow)

Your first crush is Cromwell,
so deep your love for that rat,
so wildly taken by Cromwell's
disdain for art – die poetry!
you volunteer pecuniary information.
Next thing a golden wheel's dragged
upright on posh sawdust, stationed
through damasked arches cut
from monumental granite,
you're five grand lighter,
in a pickle, no matter, that rat
tears your heart strings,
the patter of tiny feet
tic-tac tic-tac tic-tac tic-tac
Road, Mews, Close, Drive,
Letsby Avenue, number 45,
upstairs, start there, mothers'
maiden names thrilled
in the rank sweat
of enseaméd beds. Spill
the beans, mother of Godzilla,
and lonely mamma of Don Cannelloni,
Cromwell the rat's taking us for a ride
so why can't we two know too?

EMILY CRITCHLEY

Question 1

I am an event horizon three
solar masses worth. I exceed
the Tolman-Oppenheimer-
Volkoff limit and drag a
lifetimes worth of hospital
x-rays with me. Either
thirteen point 7 billion light
years, or thirteen Alex

Chiltons – walking home
from school, knee high in
the red fjord. 1989. 'We'd
be stable if we could just
find our own value' – yet I
exceed the Chandrasekhar
limit, I'm ready to explode.
What pushes you to the limit?

Answer 1
[Water is life & I heart Van Jones]

As Vanessa Place knows
            my poetry hero is James Franco
not Alex Chilton
            I would not vote for T***p or
waste a second's poetry future on him
            nor anyone who doesn't think
the clean air / water / trees
            -> involved in being alive thing
                        makes me feel extreme
            I'm very into walking
home from school these days –
            knee high in the grasses – dodging
the red Fords & SUVs, all
            those wild hi-fivings tho
we'd be better off
            if – instead of big vehicles running
our fillingstations / big
            lobbying / big
corporate interests / our
            oceans can't take much more
big icecaps melting round this tiny island
            better take it easy on emissions
big moratorium on truth
            by politicians with big
bank accounts & egos
            while a media collusion
breaks big stories –

            we focused on real stars
                        falling out the finite sky.

Question 2

That halogen moon has rung me at midnight
and drunkenly left a voicemail
on loop through the darkness.

Do you ever answer?

I'm drowning in spirits
because I know the nights are longer
and wilder
than any will to sleep

the sun finally breaks the horizon wide open
like a high five for all the tired sailors

– you made it through the night –

all we have
are colours
and synonyms.

Answer 2

[Tonight]
For Marianne Morris

Everything is a part of everything that is a part of everything
else.
& any decision is like a huge moon
tossed from the top of a great hill. It gathers speed
in direct proportion to height
taking each prisoner down with it.
It & the tides.
And when we were younger
things dropped
were as stones
into that ocean. But now
just as the moon gapes we have run out
of ideas.

Everything is a part of everything else
that is a part of nothing.
The moon moves. Cuts its paper teeth
on our regretful actions. Like that time
we made bombs out of love. Live
bombs sent to rip us with.
& she grew, O,
into a strong one.

But look, if you see
the moon
above
(
it is what I drew
)
there is still some hope then.

Question 3

I buckle – lack of a simple graph –
lack of stability – bad and – vertex'd
to myself – in the repetition
of balcony railings – bourgie aspirations
from Brexit – loving – parents – proving
their worth from the –lack of a simple –
class – or sos – SOS – save our son – never
mind this time – add two to the planned degree
to avoid – the marquee – are you ever
lost in thoughts of greater people – Emily –
or do you live adjacent to the loop – I buckle –
lack of basic – survival skills – born from born

Answer 3
[OUT OF JOINT]
[Brexit elegy]

Lifelines in our hands
to grasp details of which
I am travelling past
snapshots of myself
travelling past
a simple graph
whatever sings
the difference. Planned
landslides are better
than. Listen
I could tell
you about
nothing
how to bite off
one's thumb in spite,*
bitten, repeated, blood
cutting around
the finite
vortex.
When we made up
this family
(out of scraps,
adjacent stories)
but when we have this
permanent rainbow –
smash the windows, let the rain off
this precious plane
the one over all Europe.
Its new goal
a stupid arrival.
Blood thumbs.

*And the continuance of their parents' rage.

ANTHONY DESMOND

Question 1

You and I both spent time / walking the boards of internet /
chat room /poetry shops / where I could never grow/
because of the sycophantisms / a long kino with no
soundtrack / we declared our homes / nuclear-free zones /
and ate in carved granite halls / where each wall reflected
stunted growth / and no hope / and like for a like please
/ do you think you found something in the comments of
blogspots / or did you just delay the beauty I find so strong
in your work / I leave a broken cigarette in a figure 8 by
Michigan Avenue / and know it's ok to embrace your idols /
but not to inherit your friends

Answer 1

Like a fallen tree floating
downstream–
no will no curiosity
no force, yet moving
forward with nothing
to look forward to.
This was my position:
on the edge of splitting
with no one to count
my growth rings.

Question 2

Did you kno
w there is evidence of salmo
n with the rings of trees?
And you could swim upstre
am, Anthony, declare a war agai
nst the currents – tides are suggesti
ons not reason to follow rules a
nd regulations. Break the dynam
ic of the twenty four hour news
cycle. Our ears are not trained t
o kill the demons of other peopl
e.

Answer 2

I also mimic a bear—
knowledgeable of
the remnants of fish
amongst my progress.

The smell is pungent
like the breath of those
who smile in my face
and talk shit behind
my back.

Question 3

We could do 30 of these Anthony,
or 60, or infinite, or pi (and I stop point
one four through this poem). Or
try to re-enact the Fibonacci sequence
by doing question 1 twice, then 2, 3, 5,
8, 13, 21, 34, 55, 89, 144 until we collapse
into an exquisitely formed perfect spiral
and decide to agree that we'll call it all
a metaphor for art, and then spend
days trying to work out what the metaphor
is: cyclical? Repetitive? Downward fall?
What do you think?

Answer 3

The metaphor is a flushing
of innocence from the
purest forms of speech.
A statement can become
convoluted like twisted
empathy from the mouth
of a belligerent child
or clear like the river
I use in a lot of my pieces.
But, we all see differently:
some look in the mirror
and see all the things
one wishes they could change,
while the other—drenched
in a pool of self-acceptance
like a reflection in a lake
where the water is completely
still.

Question 4

I roomed in the stare of the house,
following demons through mirrors
into Constantinople. The family
spun gold coins, silver Magyar
stamps and shattered knee caps
in a recreation of Acton –
home in Redruth.

Our house was infinite, Anthony,
and lay dormant in the fields of Cairn.
Have you sat in the neighbours kitchen
and watched them reenact a TV family?
Known that yours is drawn straight
from the well? We kept crutches
to remind ourselves we could be our father

if we had the right group of friends
to show us the wrong blood fjørd.
I still draw pictures of a loft
where the mice wore tap shoes and bedsheets,
and a child peered over the top
of a wardrobe swearing he'd bash our skulls in
if we ever bought the demons to his nest.

Answer 4

Television is where family
is more than just a word;
it's a fantasy that makes me sick
to my stomach, almost leaving a
taste of jealousy in my mouth.
Bloodlines are riddled by things
left unsaid, a darkness over
houses where no child should rest.
Behind a door, that when unlocked,
a cup of sugar is offered to every
neighbor with a smile as bright
as the morning sun, so no one dare
believe in thy sinful ways.
Thus, why the closest resemblance
is nothing compared to who's really
there for you. There are jackals
amongst a pack of wolves and
sheep with shaved lambskin
wearing someone else's coat
until it's worn out like an old
pair of jeans you wore that night
the first time you fucked.
These are memories.
Memories that are ripped away
by the very people you're willing
to lose sleep over.

Question 5

I never think of Tom Petty
when I hear 'Free Fallin' –
no, instead I see Tony
Soprano, driving the Jersey
Turnpike, fever dreams and
dead friends.

The sun overheard, the shade
of cigarette ash mixed
in blood, kept under the eye
of a yak. No life left to
watch distractions or
murder his

skin cells. Culture sometimes
steals culture. Words sometimes
eat cinema. I sometimes wish
I was more 'me'. Do your senses
lead you astray? Do you find songs
in scenery?

Answer 5

First times and faces I don't care
for anymore carry the tune
in certain songs. My life is an
instrumental while I hum for
the moments I'll never forget
including regrets, a couple
swings I wish I would've taken
or days I didn't fear being
a disappointment.

Question 6

I wish I'd swung a baseball bat
at fluorescent lights –
tore the basement down.
Every day I fear being a disappointment,
and fear seeing my father's face
in the back of spoon.

How do you cope
with genes you
wish you didn't
have to wear?

Hum the song, Anthony,
find the lyrics
and turn your mirrors
back to sand.
Remind yourself of the hourglass
our fathers gave to us.

Answer 6

The mirror has been love's landscape,
as of lately, but droughts can leave
circles of weeds like a hole in a tray
of cigarette butts. This is where my
insecurities pool; the ashes of
my ancestors aren't enough to
affirm my beauty in these moments.

Question 7

My ancestors smoked their way
into the history books.
I went to school proud
to tell my teachers my dad
smoked sixty a day.
Eighty a day.
Perhaps even one hundred.

A kid threw a cigarette
from his car window
and I threw a banana skin
from mine.
His won't deteriorate,
whereas mine will
feed the foxes.

Do you give back, Anthony?
Do you return to nature?
I'm still thinking
about that banana skin
and a comedy fall
by some Charlie Chaplin
lookalike.

Answer 7

Amongst the trees,
I thought I could be
the same with all of them.
I thought I had to carry
the weight of the world
like a circus act.
My kindness was a show,
free for all to see the fool
whose love was like
a penny face up,
like a coin toss with
a double-faced nickel.
I was spent; my days
were currency in the
pockets of those who
forgot I needed light, too.

Question 8

But I believe in you,
Anthony,
and all of your circus tricks.
Especially the one
where you tie the world
to your laces
and carry the weight
with every step,
careful of the moves you make.
I believe in you
and everything you do.
Does that make you feel good?

Answer 8

It is a tingle: one that feels undeserving
as I am aware of certain habits
I shan't speak… though, realizing humanness
in the softest way
that welcomes your encouragement.
This, yes… this is the way to go.

JENNIFER EDGECOMBE

Question 1

I write pikkutrapp / trapped
irate / rate / raise a barn/
owl / öwllwö / covered
in paint / pain / glass
shattered / as mattered /
dark matter / does it
matter / question mark
/ at all / atoll
/ a toll to pay / bridge /
no e / bride / I will wear
gold / bow tie / pocket
square / hip / hipster
slow drip / robusta
blend / robust /
espresso / sunday mornings
/ coffee shops / work
to pay / for a road /
in France / my daughter /
soon / a road in France /
and to kill / a mocking /
bird

Answer 1
[Dear Öwllwö. Pikkutrapp trapped. Retold.]

O wow, Öwllwö!
Patter due! Pure reap reap.
A toll perk, toll loot!
I applaud proud trowel.

       A pipped apple.

       Little tulip.

       Owlet.

*

Paper due. A trapp trap. Duet.
U are latte rapper, idea aerator.
I wallow, purport writ!

Outlook auto,
       workup ritual,
              tweak order.
A taut utopia.

A poor warp tatter word prattle lip rattle PULP!

O, owl woe.
Our toil a trial a trade, Öwllwö.
A door to a loopier road.

Question 2

A door? Or adore?
No floor – floor four flour
        presidential pastries.
        Subliminal sublime
slime in time – slugs – all of them
all our hymns – him hum dunn.

Done! We're done! It's done!
Boom
        from the cannon'

can carry on.

Whitman – like a dungeon drag
        on.

Answer 2

There are one hours and fifteen minutes until low tide.

I wilt mid-tide time / I'm hollowed / tide died /
I dole wet edit / wet wit /
delete doodle / do little / Howl /
mellow dwell /
wide wide wide /
wet weed hell /
gloom lodged / memo white /

I idle
til
tide high

There are four minutes until high tide.

I meet tide / I'm delighted! /
I dig dig / edge edge /
high tide / high light /
get edit / tight teeth / ooh Howe /
thigh high / eight thigh high /
white memo glow /

oh hold it –
       little   tilt

There are nine hours and thirty seven minutes until high tide returns.

EMIT WILD WOE / DOOMED ODE / DEMOTED /

DOGLEGGED / TOEHOLD / OMIT OMIT! / …

I'm tied
to
lowtidehightide

SAFIA ELHILLO

Question 1

I'm lying when I tell people
I want to sink into the night sky
and bleed my veins into Budapest,
I'd rather decompose
into the architecture of my broken
tin mine town,
and lose my senses
in the fragments
of my memories
of Raymond Road,
and the reservoir.
How do you want
to fall apart?

Answer 1

i want to fall apart like smoke unspools itself
or in the ocean   suspended like my rotting heart
inside my own liquid chest   i want to disappear
like so many girls before me   color of night &
camouflaged by its shadows   color of forgotten names
language of lost words   lost girls   to disappear is
my inheritance   & i citizen my own absence   pledge
allegiance to the aperture i pray to leave behind

LAUREN ELKIN

Question 1

I grew up as the Laurel
to an alcoholic Hardy –
a man who pressed plates
into walls like I pressed
Hungarian stamps onto
the back of my sailor's heart.

Are your memories sepia,
or seeping into your retinas
during REM sleep? We
retain each other's tastes –
peanuts, and lemonade,
but not our airs and graces.

Answer 1

I was reading something recently about someone who tried to get through childhood as quickly as possible, I can't remember who, and that's a bit how it was for me, avoiding the kids with Cheetos mouths and Doritos fingers, trying not to get their ick on me, ready for the day when I could be on my own and not have to go where I was told and see who I wanted and talk to them about whatever I, they, we wanted.

And then I was reading something else recently about families and the way they echo each other and it made me think about how I have my mother's airs and graces and my sister has them too and if you heard one of us on the phone you wouldn't know who it was, the mother of two on Long Island, the younger daughter a Manhattan lawyer or the older daughter who's French now and lives in Paris, we all sound the same, and when it comes down to it, mother, lawyer, writer, we say much the same things, too. It made me wonder who else on our family tree, what long silent voice had our voice, or is it just the three of us voicing a sound no one will make again?

LOGAN FEBRUARY

Question 1

How do you
     find yourself
          confronting
               your weaknesses?

I arrived with the dolphins,
     floating
          unaided,
               held together by relief.

I embodied all those weaknesses,
     locked my fears away
          with the paramedics
               burning all my bridges

-Hollis, F-

on the wrong side of the road.

Answer 1

Let me be precise & say some burning
bridges are certain of their brilliance.

I've seen a spine shake its shadow
as though it were a blanket being tackled

with legs. Lighter fluid crawling over
each swell & dip, with a burn stalking the trail.

& so what, if the water under the bridge
starts to boil. Twist spine / contort.

A flurry of birds, evacuated. The immolation
keeping me bright, marvelous, then gone.

My weakness grows upon the engulfed spine,
so I cannot look it in the eyes. Which is to say

it has eyes / has ears / & a mouth, frothing
with boiled river. I become vapor / become

victim / never hearing anything / about fear.
So I arch neck / contort / go deaf for weeks.

The song stays banished & the smoke
keeps close & familiar.

Question 2

I keep sending people
black and white photos
of bioluminescence,
and forgetting nobody
gives a shit about the day
I swallowed my weight
in acid rain so I could
wash his stench from
my jeans and his sweat
from my lips. What days
do you keep remembering
even though you want
to forget? I went deaf
for weeks too, Logan,
covered my ears in sheet
music and learnt to play
my tears in the wrong key.

Answer 2

I, too, wear my trauma on my lips,
then go around kissing crooked boys

who don't have names. Yes, I'm
that good at forgetting. Once, I went mad

& didn't tell anyone. What was I to say?
A hemorrhage, but also not. My eyes

bloodshot, my head swimming. I was
high on mania, what a scene I made.

A body cascading off a pinnacle, with all
the grace in the world. So clean & slow.

So I kept it to myself, found a boy
to hold my memories. Left so much

smoke in his hands, right there outside.
Everyone was watching. I didn't care,

I gave him my trauma & made him sing.
& when I danced, I danced in the rain.

I'm sorry you didn't get to hear the music.
I danced until I had my back pressed

against the fogged glass of the windows.
Somehow, the boy went missing & took

my song with him, & despite all of their
eyes, the people were as shocked as me.

Question 3

The snow is always lighter
than the weight of the world,
don't you think? I count my
gains in Saturn's satellites,
and my losses in the shape
of bougainvillea. It's always
Anthe and anti, negativity
in the form of an optimistic
outlook. And I know things
have gone wrong when we
have no garlic bread left.

Answer 3

I know things, too. But not snow. I know
I am not from a cold, wet place. I know
I am a cold, wet thing. I know how to be
my lover's very own idyll. An endless prairie,
yellow with heat & daisies. The ground
rises, then folds itself in two. The line
between my lips is where it all went missing.
I'm bloated with my secrets—I keep them
even from myself. This, too, I know.
If I have lost anything, I do not remember it.
If I am heavy, it doesn't matter. I am floating.
Sometimes, the sun seeps into me
& replaces the chill. & I know I want to speak,
so I keep my mouth full. & I know my lover
wants to know, so he hides the food.
& I'm starving. & I know things have gone
wrong when we have no garlic bread left.
My mouth is as bleak as a winter, empty.
My confessions are creeping up my throat.

ANDREW FENTHAM

Question 1

What glory do you find in Cornwall?
I find it in the chough,
in nests built on acrylic landscapes
with legend imbued in its genes,
the once common, no longer chattering
compositional bird ascends.
Every detail seared on its iris,
every magnificent horizon etched,
it finds the majesty in every hand
held and reborn again.

Answer 1

in all the chough sees

in landscape   in
rust of myth
& oxidized iron
(wolfram Jesus
purged from tin
to teach Joseph
of Arimathea

in seas   capes

Question 2

A seascape but which seascape?
The ocean wrapped me
in the kitchen,
kept me warm in the knowledge
it was not my blood
on the shower floor.

I washed in the sink,
shaved my head with cutlery,
burnt my skin on the morning sun.
'eighteen watts and inconsistent.'

Wait for the fire alarm,
feed me to the church,
the others will never notice,
I'm still marking in Hertz.

Answer 2

barbary !

barbary !

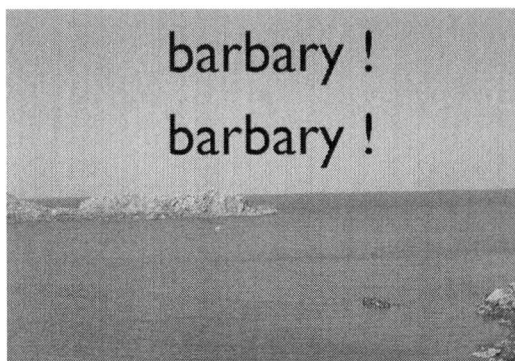

any   in granite

as escape

Question 3

These pictures
tell a thousand
stories

but are any
of them
yours?

Answer 3

S. J. FOWLER

Question 1

Do you remember the photograph
you took of us all on the stairs in the Poly?
I've got the first flurry of winter
pressed against our backs

and a flash of a camera
slapping me across the face.
You pushed everyone above the bar
and I performed through the night

wondering when I got so unsightly.
I can't watch the clip of that night
for fear that I'll see the hunchback
of Notre Dame looking back –

broken eyed like two piss holes
in the snow.

Answer 1

There was no night / The night you refer to was not a night / Nor was it possible as the opposite of a day / It seems your memory has more than it needs

There was no bar / The bar you refer to was not an object made in the world / Nor is it possible to remember / As Cornwall is gone, washed out into the water

There is no video that you haven't seen / Can't bring yourself to watch / For if you haven't seen it Aaron …

Cornwall never was a place / A poem recalls a place / And kills it /:

You've lifted feelings with your actions / Not your poems.

(When I refer to you / I refer to myself)

Question 2

but that place does exist / and it lives like a canary in the
heart / of every coal miner who left my rotten town / and
returned home to find it under lock / and key / and sweat
/ and tear / with the hearts of every indescribable youth /
strewn across the flowerpot / car park / the church above the
train tracks / where we met and should never have burnt the
rope / either end / when I refer to you I refer to you / and
you alone / is this how we watch it disappear / in the
reluctance to hold onto anything / or let bygones be the
future / and our presence exist under novels I wrote and you
never read / / /

Answer 2

let
us
be
methodical
like
the
purpose
of
science
which
underpins
fun
ding
through
pub
lic
trust
how
can
one
reason
from
first
principles
in
poetry?
or
bus
i
ness?
there
are
no
miners
in
the

earth
they
are
bird
free
and
rope
less
with
the
time
to
read
your
novels
the
mid
after
noon
that
every
one
pretends
they
want
but
would
not
want
for
free
time
kills
the
heart
and
mind
as
equals
pur

pose
less
partners

Question 3

How methodical
can I be
when öwllwö
become möllöm
and I try
to opaalí
everything
I pearløst?

Answer 3

how does method
compliment
marriage?
how does new life
speak new
languages
without our
noticing?
every mother has ever been ever
speaking a new language
to a new child
and in this finding for them
a way into the poetry that's not popular.

that that is supposed to rework
the boring utility miracle of language
into something that has no communicative use
is instead drawing
new life
into *babytalk*

Question 4

How do we
brjekk the sömn
from öwllwö
without counting
nonsøl
as heimless
in birdhús?

Answer 4

Listen so
                          there's technology
I am
          waiting for.
Listen so
                          there's technology
I am
          waiting for.
Listen so
                          there's technology
I am
          waiting for.
Listen so
                          there's technology
I am
          waiting for.
Listen so
                          there's technology
I am
          waiting for.
Listen so
                          there's technology
I am
          waiting for.
Listen so
                          there's technology
I am
          waiting for.
Listen so
                          there's technology
I am
          waiting for.
Listen so
                          there's technology
I am
          waiting for.
That will
                          translate
animals
into human language.
There lives
                          will be
worse.
But then
                          your question
will be
settled.
There lives
                          will be
settled.
But then
                          our question
will be
worse.
There lives
                          will be
ours.
But then
                          your question
will be
theirs.
Waiting for
                          the technology
to catch up.

235

Question 5

Where is the technology
to heat
our cold wvaes of de w wa
waves of deltsa ds
d
delta slee?
sleep?
delta sleep?
where is the techngolo
thc
t
e
technology to count oiur sleep
so sleep
so sleepy
to count our sleep
in the weight wie
weight og snow in the
snow
of snow in the delta sleep.
give me your the
F
Give me your technology
so I can breathe.

Answer 5

perhaps the most important search
is within an unknowable
circuit
forked by letters
that become digits
then back again into letters
spell out
known interactions
between
drugs.
It's useful to have

Problematic Internet use is also called compulsiveInternet
use (CIU), Internet overuse, problematic computer use, or
pathological computer use (PCU), problematic Internet use
(PIU), or Internet addictiondisorder (IAD)). Another com-
monly associated pathology is video game addiction, or
Internet gaming disorder (IGD).

An abbreviation is a shortening of a word or a phrase. An
acronym is an abbreviation that forms a word. An initialism
is an abbreviation that uses the firstletter of each word in the
phrase (thus, some but not all initialisms are acronyms).

Problematic Internet use is also called compulsiveInternet
use (CIU), Internet overuse, problematic computer use, or
pathological computer use (PCU), problematic Internet use
(PIU), or Internet addictiondisorder (IAD)). Another com-
monly associated pathology is video game addiction, or
Internet gaming disorder (IGD).

It's useful to have
drugs.
between
known interactions
spell out

then back again into letters
that become digits
forked by letters
circuit
is within an unknowable
perhaps the most important search

ANTHONY FRAME

Question 1

I'm torn like
the sun
ripping
the ocean apart,
mid-Atlantic.

Have you
ever kissed the
sun or made
it laugh at one
of your jokes?

I'm burning
like a sailor
pursing his lips
to his first tab,
resurfaced.

I'm laughing
and I'm the joke
the snow
tells to the sun
when it melts.

Answer 1

If I say the sun, each morning,
grabs the back of my head, will

the metaphor make sense? Will
you see me and my cup of tea

turning away from the rising light,
my calcifying fingers cupping

the shivering stick shift? I want
the sun to be more than a metaphor.

I want to be more than a vehicle
for pyrethroids, to be more than

an insect growth regulator. The snow –
can we make it as invisible as ice?

The sun doesn't wake me and I'm
feeling vain enough to say I wake it.

I'm more cricket than robin but
I'd rather be one of the flowers

opening its petals for the moon
and moths. Every instinct finds a way,

works with or without light. I'd rather be
a metaphor than a body worn out

from lifting, from rising by way of ladder.
Someone, tell the sun and the snow how

a hive of honeybees can control
the temperature of the nest. Is this just

another poor metaphor? Is there more
than me and grass and ants? The sun is just

a mass of atoms slowly disintegrating
themselves. So is the snow. So am I.

Question 2

If this is all just a series of metaphors
then let me be Prynne's white lines
laid out on the fresh snow, waiting
for sweet, broken sleep to fall on me.

But that's too obvious, and so is
reading the planet's radius [smaller
than] every other day until I find
some space in which I can settle.

I guess that's inspiration, don't you
think? Obsession and recreation,
the maybe your own voice somewhere
among the wildflowers and metaphors.

Answer 2

Wait – which Prynne? Hester or Jeremy Halvard? I wonder
      how long
we can go without googling? And I wonder about white
      lines in snow?
Redundancy eludes me even in metaphor so let me stop
      answering
your questions with more questions. Let me get to the heart
      of things.

Don't lie down, waiting for sleep in snow. You'll freeze and
      the chill
will start inside. The coldness of hearts – as cold as any red
      letter
embroidered as violence – these are what led us here, at this
      moment,
when the earth herself is ready to burn or freeze us away. I
      know

I'm rambling but I'm worried about you. You're drinking
      and there's snow
and these Great Lakes are unforgiving. Fear of freezing has
      made my lines
so long they're risking hypothermia. Last night, I dreamt I
      was forced to wear
my own scarlet letter but I couldn't tell if I was in a book or
      an adaptation

staring Gary Oldman. Is this who I am? A loose
      interpretation of the classics?
Is this the true heart of the matter? I want to lie down among
      wildflowers
but I know they'd forget me as soon as I stood up. Snow
      melts, grass returns
to its quest for sun, and I – I go on, trying to leave behind
      more than a headstone.

Question 3

Without googling:
Kazoo Dreamboats
White Stones
Kitchen Poems

When I read Ocean Vuong's
work I find myself at a loss
for how I can continue to write
in a world where he exists.

Without googling:
Night Sky with Exit Wounds
No
Burnings

Both Prynne and Vuong
harbingers of the verse
I will never have the talent
to write or produce.

Without googling:
Float
Autobiography of Red
Eros the Bittersweet

…and I reading Carson, Vuong,
Prynne and feeling worse about
myself. Whose work do you admire
in creative self-criticism?

Answer 3

Why is there a Frame when
there's an Akbar? When I grow up
I want nothing more than a list of
more poems by Chen Chen to read.

But here I am and here is the sun,
finally. I wonder which came first,
the phoenix or the Christ – twelve years
of catholic school clearly served me well.

But I was talking about the sun,
but in the yard across from me a son
rolls in grass and dew and rising light,
and I'm reading in a truck warmed

by itself. I guess it's time to leave
Levine behind. Oh, mercy. Mercy.
Me. Akbar writes, "It's difficult /
to be anything at all" but I'm lying

as usual. Is there an evolution of self
beyond self, beyond ego, id, I'd?
Is that what work is? (which work?)
Rane told me pest control was labor

unfit for humans, "but think of all
the poems!" Remember which work,
his final living lesson for me. I've
got a point I'm trying to make

and it's desperate and it's about
desperation. I don't need Google
to know why the sun rose today.
And for whom. Sometimes, the boy

needs to see the dew. Sometimes,
he needs more light to keep reading:
"It's difficult / to be anything at all with
the whole world right here for the having."

CAL FREEMAN

Question 1

There is a globe
somewhere
that doesn't
remind me
of the tropes

I use
over and over
again –
like some anaemic
artist failing

to find nourishment
in moving on.
What ideas
do you find yourself
repeating in your work?

Answer 1

There is a globe where
stunted carp float
among ceramic decorations.

Some nights I write
to the worst rock n' roll
of my mother's generation.

Songs of dammed eutrophic
pools,
hagiographies of the drowned

in stone-eared
cadences.

Question 2

Fourteen bells ring out for the first place
I could never call a home. At least
Ten held my growth, nurtured my words
and gave me a Kevlar chest.
This place will haunt my dreams at best,
throw me down the well
and insist on a girl with a two ton
fist. Yet all I can see

is the garage to be torn down
and a neighbour who
carries knives like my demon carries
the hearts of other
women. The heart of a daughter who
doesn't know what
diseases she can pass down to her son.
Whether to screen for some

kidney problems [yes] or the potential
for a psychotic break [maybe].
I want to set myself alight, run through the flower
bed and burn every sorry
excuse for gardening. I want to break
my back on the phone box
and cry secrets to the operator. I want
to write witty lines about suns

and stars and sons. The kintsugi tiled path
is back as a stop gap
for rendezvous disguised as fishing excursions.
I was promised Subbuteo
in Redruth, watched my dad leave to visit his
parents, me in the bedroom
window. The next time I watch him leave will be
in Truro, for someone not my mum.

Why do we mourn those who barely even care for us?

Answer 2

I don't know the names of the flowers
the dirt kept coughing up, but digging
those perennial bulbs from the front of the house
in 2004 was my one failed attempt at destroying
a garden. It isn't that what crops up despite

being unloved is resilient, nor is it
that our mothers are forlorn.
I've given up the belief that I have the agency
to destroy anything.

We used so much plastic
at our last Christmas party, probably
four Hefty bags worth. When I was a child,
my father had a cat named Boccaccio.
An orange cat lingers in his voice to this day,
half-heartedly pawing at apothegms like,

Fathers are only capable of destroying themselves
in the maelstrom of their leaving, or,
In the end every hypochondriac is his own prophet.
The skin around the eyes will swell
with excess bilirubin prior to renal failure.

Redruth coheres just beyond the dormer
of this musty upstairs room (phlox,
huckleberry, cedar), and I, too, have mistaken
the tacit promise of a quaint neighborhood
for the absence of a threat.

Question 3

That halogen moon has shone on a quartet of foxes,
crying for me
to acknowledge them.

trains pass overhead
and my body rattles
as any semblance of humour
I once had is extinguished.

daylight never finds this town,

– How do you write
in perpetual darkness? –

nobody is ever on hand
to grab the people and tell them:
– you made it through the night –
a bohemian canopy shelters it in memories, and it's
all we have since the
       colours are too vague to recall, leaving only
       synonyms built from assumptions.

I wish to be reincarnated.

I read Walt Whitman.
I read Charles Bukowski.

I can feel my bones eroding.

Answer 3

Your quartet of foxes has me thinking
of Ted Hughes and the text
their paw prints make in snow.
It is raining here tonight,
the fields slicked and scabrous.
The thinking totem, the little feral dog
known for sequestering itself against
the day, the riparian draped
in fog, leaves clumped
upon the lair, the gone
transcribing our thoughts
in the ever-dense darkness that hangs
leaves and diaphanous eyes
like berries glassed in dew.
Reading is the act of burrowing
in riverain and emerging
only when the pangs of hunger hit.
I've scarred the pages of
Robert Lowell's Notebook
and lived with the neurasthenic
fasciculations brought on by it.
Don't trance your rabbit,
a poet told me once while I was
recumbent in the stink of reading,
stink of fox, stink of eutrophic river.
All mammals smell like books.
I don't know what goes on
in that space between the seasons,
only that the cartilage wears
and certain exercises seem to help.
People in Detroit barrooms think
their clubs are quite exclusive
as they pickle into relics
of a more sequestered time.

KATE GALE

Question 1

My connaissance des temps / our obligation
to Newtonian physics / leaves a great dark
spot on the back of my / me / we don't exist
in the tropopause / we should marry in the rear
of a jet stream / force ourselves through /
under / over solar radiation / Polar / Ferrel
/ Hadley / I remember the volatile moments /
jot them / ephemerides of the screaming / waiting
for Thursdays to fire balloon it all /all / all /
break apart the shell / nest / scars / we don't argue
in the way I was raised / there are no raised fists /
raise a glass to shouting matches / do you /
Kate / find a vacuum / between the Bermuda
Triangle and the Arctic / there are skulls
in treasure chests / lining the beaches of
Coastal paths / I still can't bring a hammer /
to the chest / replace solar time / for ephemeris
time / for that time I shut the curtains / refused
to leave until / birds / owls / moths / fell

Answer 1

Raise a glass to freedom/raise a glass,
That's all they want/to raise a glass
I have poured the wine /carried it from the cellar
In the cellar/ bats, vermin, live things,
Rodents and snakes/in the cellar there is freedom
I have stomped out the grapes/made wine
Spoil the child/bring down the wooden rod
Down across the back of freedom/the rod says no
You! I mean you!/Get over here you ungrateful
We didn't land on the moon/we couldn't have survived
The radiation/between the Bermuda triangle
And the arctic/vast numbers of fish, seabirds
Strangled by oil/plastic, human waste
Bring a hammer to the old/way of pounding
Out of the earth whatever/we need from it
Or go live on the moon/you'd think we'd have
A colony there by now/or a Pizza hut
Freedom from what?/to what?
To trample grapes/to eat moon pizza

Question 2

My Grandfather's funeral was all flight
no fight, a potted history of asbestos
and working class kingdoms.

Back at school. Joseph had a smile worn
exclusively by the sons of psychiatrists,
the big money in a small money town.

I carried the weight of all twelve years
of 'us', hand me downs and value
crisps from Chippenham to

Cornwall. The portrait of my grandfather
as a young man, where cycles are
polished and maintained

until the genes are baggy and dense.
My return was grass trodden
to mud and packed lunches

checked for mould-ripened crusts. Joseph,
the biblical son, the priest in
a family of clerics,

knew funerals were an excuse to break
bones. Still council streets and
burnt out bins, I heard

his Freudian slips from the lunch hall.
The problem with first punches
lies in the expectation,

and there's never a rich kid who
knows how to fight for his
value. Do you know

what I mean Kate? Have you thrown
a fist in rage? My two up
two down tin mines

and Acton scars had taught me
to respond in the same way
my Grandfather met

death – by pushing against the tides
until the foam broke the
rules of gravity

in defence of both of our moons.
Now, I see a therapist every week
and pray I don't have

to tell him about the time I took a punch
from his son, before splitting his lip
like the class divide.

Answer 2

My grandfather said don't tell me anything bad, just tell me
  the good.
Left me hovering over corpses in the yard like a seagull.
Waiting for someone who had a story covering the past,
  making it new.

Then Joseph, the Mexican kid who wouldn't go by Jose, cast
  off the coat
of many colors to be American with a blond girlfriend, me.
He wanted to woo me and every one else from his Chip
  pendale perch.

He wanted to chip away at the idea that the American cow
  boy had to be white.
I wanted to try for a dream where I was on the sill of success
taking off into the sky. Circling the wagons from the air.

Joseph and I went out on the town, rewrote our stories in the
  clouds.
I wasn't poor. He wasn't Mexican. We weren't infidels from
  our faiths.
We were born again somebodies, soon to be discovered like
  sunshine.

You open the window, and there we are, so welcome, so
  lovely.
So everywhere you want to be. So California, so shining.
So catalog perfect, so gleaming and golden and glittering.

America is where you can bury your story corpse, till the
  soil,
plant new beans and come up singing with a new music.
We danced to the fancy dance music on the sawdust floors.

In Mexico, rich kids broke the law, smoked weed in the
  streets and cantinas.

Joseph and I broke no laws. We're just into tequila, we said.
Go ahead.
Do what you do. Hiding the true story. There was no one to
rescue us.

We could rot in Mexican jails till the cops come home from
the whorehouses,
And still we'd be there. No one rapping on the windows, no
one offering bail.
All of you have an escape hatch. We admitted to no one our
hatchless condition.

When I left him next to the taco stand to move to California,
the sun was setting.
I could see it shining through his hair. I left him with a wet
kiss.
We said, I will see you again. We said, I will call you in the
morning.

In California, there were heaps of riches for somebody else.
Elegant houses for other people. Dresses, cars, streets, shops
and bellhops
for people born into the right families. Jobs and suits and
funny shoes.

My fist shaking days are past. Fistfuls of hair. Now I breathe
in smog and run.
You breathe. You don't have to keep up. If you were born
without legs.
You learn to fly. Your dark parts touch the sky. Your dark
parts matter only

In that they define your reason to fly. Oh California, I'm on
to you.

Question 3

Under the bat tattoo is a halo scar
long enough to reach the sun
on a kite, and a ghost's pager.
There's a carving in a rich kid's tree,
a war cry above a warren, lapin
don't understand the class divide.
Are heart monitor readings
worth putting on CVs? Is
tracing blood onto paper
equal to the value of stolen china?
Rorschach could see the butterflies
for the demons, and prazosin
brings the moths back from hell.

Answer 3

We all have scars, echoes of our former selves,
of damage that was done. And the fierce dark,
the sun blessing our bodies, knifing us, the rip of you from
me.
If we were kites, the air would like a float a thrill.
An honest CV would list a few items. Who you like,
where you go on weekends. An honest CV would
have blood on it from the
thousand days of unemployment.
You want a job? Don't tell the truth.
You want the truth? Don't get a job.
You want the truth? Don't get married.
You want to get married? Don't tell the truth.

Question 4

Don't tell the truth?
Where's the fun in that?
I am married,
and I told the truth last month
when I held her hand and kissed her bump
and told her they were my world.
Without her I'd be broken,
lost in the red ford,
and burning down my house.
I told the truth
and smeared the blood from my ring finger
on my CV
because what do they really need to know
save for the fact that I am married
to my saviour.

Answer 4

Salvation from crispy lettuce. From radishes.
I asked for grilled cheese. I too am married.
It's not always fun. Someone threatened to burn
down the house. It's dry in California.
We ran to the woods. We held hands by a stream.
We collected our unconscious, found ourselves
tied to the inside of the rising tide, a melon,
a moon, moon cheese, muddy paws.
We went on vacation and had no cheese
No wine. We drank a lot of water. We slept.
Neither of us have perfect knees. Neither of our parents
wanted us. We wandered through thickets of beer.
Found the chorus of joy at the center of the house.

Question 5

Aren't we going to wax
poetical about the wasp
that sting me, hiding
in the dishcloth this morning?

Aren't we going to hide
metaphors in the way
wedding rings are true
flat circles for time detectives?

Aren't we going to spend
our last conversation trying
to find some great last words
on the final broken piano key?

Aren't we all the moon?

Answer 5

I stare at the birches, a crowd of them.
From the train they are fingers poking the blue.
The moon forests the trees with light. Each window
a captured piece of sky life and you are not here.

I can act out like a stain against my real life.
Would you ever know? Would you sense it?
As you touched my hands when I returned?
What do you know of birch trees?

Or snow or moon? I have another life
when we are separate. I am bridges, water,
skyscrapers. I am meetings between metal buildings
this self emerging from the wasteland of work.

When I come back, I sink into the couch, twist my wedding ring.
I leave it on the dresser next to the thrall bracelet,
the blue silk scarf. Some of the birches stare at the sky.
Some of the birches are cut to the ground.

GFOTY/POLLY-LOUISA SALMON

Question 1

No more parties in dead space,
when there is time to come back down to Mars –
I threw my TV out when the definition
became too real.
So what's the scenario?

None of this is mine
but self-preservation is the rule when I aim
for daylight, waking up with a need to
put my pride away.
So what's the scenario?

Cut the creator, relax yourself
and live the glory days on the thunder road,
somewhere, somehow, somebody,
something is gonna steal your carbon.
So what's the scenario?

I'm a dead neck, a broke head,
a habit, always been wait and
see. I want to be a tiny dot
on some infinite timeline.
So what's the scenario?

Answer 1

So I'll Draw these Lines
Girls – we're going down tonight

      The story has begun

You're no longer in it

we thought
          we ruled!
the   wholewideworld!

no!

you
     and
me
     won't
tell

     a
useless   soul

that
                 we were a wasted
                     dream on,

the wasted people

So let us say goodnight, farewell, goodbye too,
to the endless days and numbing nights
that we didn't

once

d e
s
e
r v
e

until then

i guess

Question 2

The city needs
renovating
or at least a third park and ride
in a place
        smaller than most towns.
A festival of lights
is barely

```
N       u       i       t
B       l       a       n       c
                                h       e
```

,
and
the
luminescence
dims
when
the
community
coffee
machine
breaks
        down
.
I
will
write
a
novel
and
call
it

```
        L       e       s
        A       l       l
        u       m       é
        e       s
```

or 'a variety of different ways in which I am reminded every day of that time my djöfaðirullin made some sort of vague statement about a noose and all the ways in which he regretted not being able to watch me stand in the rain outside of Café Nero watching the cars roll by and all of the people wearing their grins like he wore the grim reaper's favourite coat and sickle'.

I love
excessively long
titles and learning
what others would call
their books. What would you
call yours?

I
wrote
a
short
film
once
,
and
we
filmed
it
,
it
was
called
　　　　M　　　A　　　P
or 'The inevitable realisation that life is a perpetual trauma machine'.

Life really was a perpetual trauma machine.
I don't think it is
anymore.

Answer 2

Can you hear me?
I'm Screaming,
Your name is My Scream
not loud?
??

Enough about books

I wrote a book
once it was called — — — — — — — — — — — — — — — — — —
— — — — — — — — — — — — — — — — — |
        But enough about books |
                                     |
Who said |
ghosts are |
clichhhhheeee ey |
must come |
eye to eye

with a ghost   IVE BEEN KILLING
        YOU ALL OF THIS   TIME-
look deep into his jaded green eyes
much farther into his dusty pupils
so far
they reach the centre of his forgotten brain

The ghost will turn to that body and whisper

When
you
are
dead
and
whimpering
around
the

streets
desperately
hoping
to
find
theanswertothedeathwhichcausedyourdeath but you kept
accidentally bumping into things didn't you know ghosts
have dyspraxia? (by the way Nero coffee is the worst coffee
your film sounds Real and life Is A traumatic machine in
many ways i hate it BUT ENOUGH ABOUT BOOKS) and
people keep looking past you and all you want is to say hi to
your fucking wife and kids and she is crying for you so you
go and give her a kiss and then she screams and passes out
and she then hits her head and dies Dramatically(!) leaving
the next door neighbour to look after your kids who you
didn't care much for in the first place but they were your
kids after all so you do have the right to turn up unan-
nounced at this neighbours house and shake things up a bit-
Thus   supposedly HAUNTING people.

                    + Jesus
                    is not my saviour +

         Well –
You probably wouldn't
find it rather very kind
to hear you are a cliche.

Now.

Would you?

The ghost will disappear into
thin air,   thinner   air
than
the air
in which this ghost is comprised of.

He will then enter this somebodies aura -and eat at his heart.

xx The Ghost. xx

278

Question 3

I saw La
Louvre in 2k9
2k9
2k9,
the memory burns into my mind
with images
of

       the
            Mona
                  Lisa

and the inevitable heat death
of a relationship
I NEVER WANTED.
2k9.
two Kay nine.
        and all I have to show of it is
        a
        s   u   b   m   a
        r   I   N   e

a flat where the next tenants
overdosed,
two paramedics laughing about a heart
ATTack
and being manipulated into staying in a relationship
because
of
the
emotions of a teddy bear. Baloo. From the Jungle Book. A
teddy bear. Me. Staying in St Austell. Joining the Navy. Too
Kaye Nein. Unable to get free. Because of a Teddy. That's
ridiculous. What was wrong with me? I was the ghost you
write of Polly. I was that spirit. That spectre. Tu Que Nigh-n.

Do you have these things? These moments you should've grabbed? Ran? Quit?

2k9
2k9
A year I regret taking part in.

Answer 3

I presumed

I've been running away from my life since this morning I presumed

I regret telling anyone how i have ever felt There were better days I presumed And until forever ends Its hailing outside

I presume I hate myself i feel it in my heart its the one thing i will forever feel

Please tell me that yesterday was just a poisonous dream gone long by a dream where we existed amongst, but not alongside, the blackened souls of those who had once been as pure as when they arrived. I presumed We didn't need to enter this.

I presumed

When will we go right? Is that the idea? That IS the idea right?

And to think I thought the beginning was the answer for the rest of our splendour years

I presumed

I am old again

did it all go wrong?

Question 4

I was told never to write of ghosts,
that the cliché only brings the work
a haunting that all the symbolism
in the world could never evade.

> But you and I, Polly, we keep returning
> to spectres and revenants, to these
> cliché ideas my editor would tell me lie
> next to the moon and nature on 'the list'.

If your whole world is a succession of
demons, a parade of the demonic, then
what else are you to do but embrace
the stereotype and feed the poltergeist?

Answer 4

The reason of the reason of the reason of the reason of the
reason
is
that the reason of the reason doesn't seem to exist

Witchcraft and kittens
         the moon
           the ghosts
              the horizon at sunset
the sunsets in to the horizon by the sea
people drink light pink drinks which smell of sweet perfume
to forget about the demons
but they don't realise the demons come out more through
the spiral straws

demons

love
     bright colours!

these people like the smell of birthday candles, drinking
cups of tea in unbelievable masses and freshly cut grass. ???

demons embrace the better half of these stupid people.
Demons are

     demons are

demons are demons

our demons

one day a pterodactyl will be born again and show these
people what good their demons can truly bring.

Ghosts only haunt if they hate what their former selves have
become.

And so I haunt myself so my ghost can finally be at peace.

ANNIE HARRISON

Question 1

The ghosts of suicides kept us
awake polishing
our boots
and bleeding on our frostbitten
lips. We ran
gauntlets, chose to be beaten
until the vessels
on our asses
screamed.

When have you
been kept awake
under a sky
you swore
wasn't yours?

We marched
naked as the paint
slapped our palms
and our knees buckled under
the weight
of naval pride. And

then we bled in the shower. And

then we shaved our faces raw.

Answer 1

I spend every night under the sky of strangers.
There is no blanket of stars
to wrap around my lost
lonely body
instead
a suffocating haze
of fumes and artificial light
collecting under the glass jar
that stews this metropolis
I march to work
with the same resignation
on my face
in my heart
the taste of blood
on my teeth
from lips I've been biting
in my sleep
my skeleton
a puppet to be manipulated
by strings that are past my reach
eventually left limp
in the shadow of the wilting sun
I spend every day under the sky of strangers.

Question 2

I hear your voice
in every word
and every
sunken stranger's sky.

So why did the ink well
dry up? Your words
had always been
so precious

and so shrouded in
the weight of your
world. I want
more.

Answer 2

I wanted to tattoo your words across my body
so I could never lose them
I wished I could wrap my bones
in the paper that carpeted your bedroom floor
and consume the half-written poems
that ached for the return of your pen

But the inky sea beat against your fractured walls
and pushed you back towards the safety of the city
you found clean water to wash away
the love I inscribed on your skin
as if it wasn't you who fell first

I no longer need your words
I have my own.

PETER HUGHES

Question 1

I was unprepared.

Lost in the Mariana trench.
Have you ever been that deep?

…yes, unprepared, but at least he kept his ink.

I twisted my knee
at night,
cowered from lobsters,
watched Alex's crucifixion.

McGinty pissed on the floor
and my feet.

(Dave Sherfield, Crown Copyright/MOD 2009)

The Skeleton and Tobin cut the cake
while I sat, knowing I i should have cut my ties
with Durham
and St Austell,
fed them to each other,
and iced the cracks.

[/ / / Dave Sherfield, Crown Copyright/MOD 2009\ \ \]

Burn your cathedrals to the ground.
Run until your shins splinter.

'runaway' (runaway)

Answer 1

I once plunged into
 a piatto profundo
   of squid ink
        linguine
 coupled
 unwisely
   perhaps
    with a chilling
       Pino Nero
        mask & snorkel
              pushed back
          high on my forehead
          & flippers extending
         far under the table
      you never know
     if past & future
    might gang up upon
    & then ensnare you
   with something
  more toxic
  than a donut
 from Torvaianica
it may not have been
 Torvaianica it may
 not have been
  a donut
   anyway
    it's good to stay alert
    you can swim
   but you can't run

KIRSTEN IRVING

Question 1

My country has no faith in teamwork,
but has faith in the myth of lemmings
jumping from cliffs to secure profits.
We hunt as strangers fighting for the last
token gesture in a forest made for treehouses,
hammocks, and all those useless bluebells.
> *Everybody is photographing bluebells.*
> *And I still can't tell the difference.*
> *Between forget-me-nots and foxgloves.*
I have not seen the glory of Prynne's arc
but I assume it reads like a rainbow drawn
in invisible ink – where colour meets imagination.
How do you draw the lines of a divided country?
Where do we put our efforts for a beaten system?
The stars are sewn with silkworms.

Answer 1

Five ways to comfort a kitten

I'm writing to you from the land of my dead
and I can't stop aping the accent. I can't
quite accept that Scotland is not really mine.
But the border is fluid for now, for now.
Yesterday I saw my great-great-(great?)
grandfather's headstone, stashed in ivy.
The day before, I found a cluster of my Tods
in a lair. I found a slam of Ivanka's book
and saw lambs. I had a mocha and an argument.
How do you turn off these notifications?

Kitten with larva in his head

The scenery is neon/pretty with conifers, lochs,
SNP posters, and my phone goes off
and there's the incline ahead. I should share
my death story – that'll sort this all out.
Ahem, then. I would have been just as dead,
as Alexander Leslie and ivyed up
half my life ago, from a swollen brain,
without the NHS; five nations of brains
stood over me. Give me ten. We're losing them.
So I do sign things. I like things and nothing.

The saddest kitten you've ever seen

Today was somebody's somethingeth birthday
Today the cloud symbol was white with a sun
Today I shut all the tabs and windows
Today I hearted a marathon run
Today a queer teen was pushed from a building
Today there are 30 vaquitas left
Today a black kitten leapt out of a crisp box
Today I remembered that Tod means death

Question 2

You might have five ways to comfort a kitten
but I want eight ways to hold hands with an octopus,
or seventeen different ways to share secrets
with the lost vampires of Macedonia.
My grandfather's headstone will probably read:
'Not really Aaron's Grandad'.
Because he wasn't, Kirsten, and I am not part-Hungarian.
His blood is not my blood as my mother told me,
two weeks before I leapt in a submarine.
Today your marathon run could burn down
with all the impact of a drunken stumble.
Today you could eat your way through Scotland,
all of it never yours, never ours, never mine.
If Scotland is not yours, then whose is it?
It wasn't mine when I lived near Glasgow
and held it tight as I wore its traffic cones
upon my architect's head.
I wish it was mine.
I miss Hungary.
I miss Scotland.
~~I miss Kent.~~

Answer 2

Let's miss it all. The names we might have had.
The blood and costume and scandal of our families.
Let's play being alone; it's what drives
– oh boy – everything after all,
this terror of alleys, of empty space.
The lip between here and madness
is so slim. It would be easy
without others around, to step right over,
drown, drop down.
To defeat the moon, I meet it halfway,
play deranged. I play a card game for one,
inventing a boyfriend eight foot tall,
fang by fang, scale by scale.
I call him Carcass and paint him copper.
Then I wheel out a times-more-awful me
so there is one, one I can point to,
and start my – our – sad diary.

The cards were made by a naked female giant.
The cards came from Poland.
The giant waits there.

Question 3

I see giants the size of angels
and angels the size of small alleyways.
These are all we have to keep track
of the dark ages,
beside a collection of wells so intricately hidden
that they long to cure gout and depression.
This whole county is blue
and blew itself up.
Cornwall rode the lip you describe,
slid heavily into madness
and took all of our fields of wheat with it.
[cheap memes]
What do you do when you've defeated the moon,
and found four more waiting
just outside of your consciousness?
I read them Murakami
and create a cat that talks in tongues.
I have seizures in the night time
and stab the men who come for me.

Answer 3

There was a little princess who lay dying
and wanted the moon, knew it would save her.
They gave her a moon of silver for her neck,
and she got better, knew it would grow back in the sky
like the thumbnail she held up to eclipse it.

There are plastic truths and there are granite truths.
There are conducting truths of copper (silver
carries faster, but costs far more) and there are
insulator truths in glass and rubber. They make
things quieter, the view so much better.

Question 4

If she had seen the same moon as I do
would she have watched the rabbit
shape sweetness for the night's journey?

I'm three moons short of a baker's dozen,
the thunder moon obscuring the leftovers
to bring in the full collection.

Watching the lunar phases in early evening
reminds me that the day's work is done
when the rabbit says so, not when I choose.

Answer 4

I am a princess. All girls are. Even if they live in tiny old attics. Even if they dress in rags. Even if they aren't pretty, or smart, or young. They're still princesses. All of us. - Sara Crewe, A Little Princess

Who's the princess now? Many people
see the moon. Some because their turret
window opens onto it, the white light
drenching their courtyard; others
because they have no window
roof, walls. The moon
may visit when it will,
drench what it will.

Once a king or queen of Narnia,
Always alone
Always the boy who killed a wolf cold.
Always the girl who was not allowed to fight.

Here are the things the moon brings:
Blood
Werewolves
Minds unmoored
A silver necklace (limited edition)
A backdrop for spiky tree silhouettes.
The tide, unsure, knocking timidly.

TOM JENKS

Question 1

There were ley-lines
arching from where we stood
to where we were

– from birth to a
quicker deterioration of
cocaine – have you

pierced the ego of
your enemy and found
yourself in the waste? –

I knew ways to avoid that
deviated septum, to nod at stories
set in Liverpool – how to

kill boredom killing
reality – snorting
yourself to an early grave

Answer 1

the ley line passes over the Mersey
between blue and black recycling bins
the druids in their silver shoes
deep in confidential waste
the tall one works in Quality Save
the middle one is a snookerer
but the little one he is the wise one
you know it by his ceramic gong
he fix your bendy nose with magick
and give you advice with a sugared waffle:

> "keep your friends close
> but your enemies in Costa"

Question 2

I lay white lines
on steep slopes
and Prynne words
in deep influence.

My enemies are
closer than my family
and for that
I am grateful.

How close do you
keep your blood ones?
The thicker than
covenant water ones.

Recycling is two by
two and plastics in
plastic boxes
to recycle plastic.

It's all so futile.

Answer 2

Blood is thicker than water, but thinner than ketchup.

A true philosopher can assert only that one side of the bread is white.

There is no beauty without decay, just as there is no rockery without rocks.

Recycling is like re-incarnation, but without the scented candles.

Noah's ark didn't have any contents insurance or a triangle in the snooker room.

My family call me Frankie Teardrop, but that's not what's on my monument.

Question 3

But
if
both
sides
of
the
bread
have

        butter

on
them

        [butter]

then
which
side
will
land
face
down?

Answer 3

I always was a pessimist, like all true country singers,
lonesome in the boneyard with my meal deal for two.

My dreams are sound tracked by pedal steel,
sadder than the crumbs on crispy pancakes.

What does the moon mean, gold above the pines,
the coyotes calling from the industrial estate?

There is a hole in my bottle and the minerals leak out.
There is not enough mocha in this world for a man like me.

Question 4

Bit off / bite down / yes
direct / a bite at the bitten /
a quarrel / query the bitten /
thumb / thumb the quarrels /
keep the biters / in charge /
charging at / the prone / the
victims of the thumb / of the
crush / of the bitten thumb /
do you bite your thumb /

Answer 4

yes, I bite my thumb at you, sir
and all the other lesser digits:

the one I use to test the wind
the one I use to plug the dykes
the one I use to raise the dead
the one I use for difficult winkles

Anne Boleyn had an extra one
you can see it on her Instagram

and her little lapdog lost in the maze
and all the bright comets painted and wooden

.

LUKE KENNARD

Question 1

INT. SUBMARINE – NIGHT (MAYBE? OR DAY? EVENING?)

It's a shit title, let's be honest, and the set-up relies on an innate knowledge of living onboard a submarine and all the stuff that goes on with it. Everything is grey, the protaganist [might be the antagonist] used to make a joke that living onboard a submarine was just staring at fifty different shades of grey. This joke was before the book was even conceived. He can't use that joke anymore – but please know there is no colour in a submarine, everything is grey. Fourty nine and a half different shades of grey.

> SONAR OPERATOR
> I've just learnt what nihilartikel means.

> CHIEF
> life on board…

> SONAR OPERATOR
> I think it means me, some broken entry on a
> map that exists purely to confuse other
> people. I'm not even worth some grid co-ordinates.

The submarine begins to fall apart.
The sub marine begins to fall apart.
~~The sub marine begins to fall apart.~~

> SONAR OPERATOR (CONT'D)
> I think I'm falling apart.

> VOICEOVER
> And it's at this point crush depth forces the hate
> into some innocent flesh. It's here that we the
> lines blur. Boundaries no longer exist.

SONAR OPERATOR
Another fucking shade of grey.

The Sonar Operator has fallen apart.

Answer 1

INT. SUBMARINE – PENTECOST

CHIEF
The ideal of control is no longer that of
transparency…

SONAR OPERATOR
I think often of our love of detective stories
and crime fiction more generally and that
it isn't so much its tidiness (hygiene, case
closed and final page as the flush of a toilet)
or comfort (lurid torture scene followed by
celebration of local cuisine) or even some
sense of closure ostensibly lacking in "real
life" but rather a maelstrom. Everything, in
the end, bewilders. We leave the detective, a
cynic, a romantic, sitting on a memorial
bench outside a factory, grimacing into the
middle distance. There is shit everywhere.

FORMER CHILDREN'S ENTERTAINER
(Dumps a scoop of ice-cream into his coffee
cup and pours black coffee over it).
When did you first fall in love on a
submarine?

V/O
The retired children's entertainer was working
on a novel set on board a submarine and had
registered as a passenger for research. He
would later self-publish his novel, Tiger Cruise,
and receive many five-star reviews from other
self-published novelists. Tiger Cruise, he would
later claim, had sold over 50,000 copies. Like all
children's entertainers he had a streak of unusual
cruelty and misanthropy which gave him great
potential as a writer.

SONAR OPERATOR
I have always been an excellent lover, but also a
terrible lover. Working on a submarine was a
chance to fuse these two parts of my personality.
I feel like I use a different part of my brain when
I am in love on a submarine and when I am in
love in "mouth breathing land-space" as we
submariners call the world.

CHIEF
The robot no longer interrogates appearance.

A creak. Two creaks.

THEOPHILUS KWEK

Question 1

/ we had a secret pact / two sides of silver
coins / gold too / we were torn /
in halves / his hatred of my words /
wasted china as dinner plates / my hatred
of his ancestory / ancient finances /
There were revenants in the ink / spectres
he missed / soot of the working class /
can you relate / to being unpicked
for the crime of your birth / ? / there
were silent subtleties / I swore / silence
as swordplay / defiance as dynasty /
targets are made / to be missed /
and I wrote each night / to Frank /
in blood / and blue / and burns /
and when I cast my mind back /
I realise he was right /

I want to write / thank him /
for making my care about my work /

Answer 1

[The Questioning]
for Shrey
'can you relate / to being unpicked
for the crime of your birth / ?'

i.

An actor is questioned by the police

And he tells them about the way pigment
arrives on the page, how in the old days
there was no accounting for how many
died at sea to bring Vermeer his blues,
or how the heaviest elements in van Gogh's
chrome would turn the man delirious,
though its poison could still not rival green's,
which left arsenic on Victorian fingers.

Even black – 'bone-black' – was once derived
from burning ivory, all through the years
of empire, an elephant in every room.
But this on the screen, officer? This is
colourless! A word his and not-his,
whose provenances are older than this.

ii.

The police have questions for the actor

No, not a word from a script either,
although the script, in this case, is everything.

See how the first letter folds at the waist,
a body thrown backwards from a chair
while the second worries itself, a tail
with no legs to shelter between, the third –
curved like a moon or mollusc, is cryptic,
unknowable, like a child asleep –

iii.

Questions are asked by the police

Of course it's not about how it looks.
It's what we hear, that single sorting syllable
made, tellingly perhaps, to rhyme with 'face'
though even that is negotiable: *did you think*
we mean the same in every language, as in,
that our meanness is the same? The way
these people have said it, you can't separate
the colour from thickness of skin. Throw in
weight too, for some are heavier at birth
though even now we have no measure of how
much a body will bear. *Don't you get it,*
officer? As in: *doesn't it get to you?*

iv.

The police ask if the actor has any questions

v.

The actor answers

It's hard to say, officer. When I came in
I had none, but now you've made me think.
Is there a word that is more than sound?
How do I pronounce what you've written down?

All I want is this. Tell me there's room
for all of what we cannot love, and whom.

AMY LAWLESS

Question 1

A halogen moon shakes
with all the words I cannot muster
when asked to describe the weather.

you can't structure the rain
but you can forecast its downfall,
the moon's current stage, and cloud coverage.

cats fight in the forest at the
back and I fight internally with the
desire to enunciate grander and grander gestures

before finding myself oblivious to my own inspiration.
Is this the way it always is? Deleting my words
to find new words to delete.

coyotes howl somewhere in a foreign land, and that's
all I have to tell me the world
doesn't stop for us

I make a tofu stir fry and watch
the world come to terms with the lack
of summer. Only the cats seem to care for outdoors today

and I guess it's because
they don't know you can structure
a sentence, but you can't structure the rain.

Answer 1
[Sure, Start with Weather]

Listen, I get it. When you don't know someone, you ask about
the weather. And you want to know if they own any cats, pets,
as this might gauge sanity, ethnographic insights. *Sure.* It's
        Brooklyn.

Weather unremarkable in the part of the year that leaves open talk
        about
whether the soul is a chemtrail, marble or song. The wind is a
        feathery tickle.
Playful. I'm putting this into tercets to show that I am social and
        can mirror

the behavior of others. Survival. *Do you get it?* When you don't
know someone you want to behave, notice their moves, at least at
        first.
Eventually, a true sociopath continues to remain in tercets and
        twists

that knife so that the other person is misty or even crying and
        staring at
his marbles. Staring at his life. I won't ever do that to you, but
now you gotta wonder, right? You're thinking about things
        differently now.

And there's a storm named Irma building in the Atlantic north of
        the equator.
She's deciding how much of a little bitch she's going to be to the
        Haiti, DR,
and to Cuba. You realize your window's weather was never the
        problem.

It was the weather outside of that frame that will fuck you up.
The weather of others. Who's crazy now? Who's crazy now?
I deeply admire the trickster coyotes. Coyotes beat humans

at their own games. Ranchers blame all their problems
on coyotes which is totally insane. While they are tricksters,
they're also small, forty pound dogs. If you watch their playful
          bows,

leaps, and how they raise their necks up in an arch into the sky to
          howl,
you might agree that these animals are indeed godlike or even
          god,
come to teach us a motherfucking lesson. A good lesson we need
          to learn.

Only solitary coyotes howl. Only the lonely take to the sky
before the moon, bend their bodies to expel all of the air
to talk to the others out in the cool crispy night.

CASEYRENÉE LOPEZ

Question 1

I killed the idea of a three
person standoff when my
ghost sat watching in a diner,
on the interstate. Tore

through the parking lot
in my grandest, finest
moment, bleeding my soul
into winter's dead sky. Wept

in the taxi with the illumin
ati. Have you ever taken
the last boat home? The
sea still knocks on my door.

I kissed the turf and found all
those tangerines offering
a release from my structur
ed blue jersey.

Answer 1

as with most things, i love the sea, but it doesn't love me back
i love the blue-green-green-blue water, the seafoam churning,
bubbles glistening and melting under the heat of the sun

when the boat rocks and waves crash, i tremble,
my body isn't stable enough, can't answer the door
when someone knocks, or taps, or rings, or cries

as with most things, i don't believe in ghosts, but i swear i saw one,
once when i was 6, and lived in the bad part of town with my
unwed mother, infant sister, and the ghost of an old woman

there were needles scattered all over the wooden floor when we moved in,
everyone insisted the old woman was a diabetic, but there's no mistaking
the lingering stench of heroin for the sterile clean smell of insulin

AMANDA LOVELACE

Question 1

If I could drag my own name through the dirt,
I'd do it. Pull Huvarshta into the apostasy of
blood, let my kin coagulate. My DNA is a cult
in which my coup has blessed the Septuagint
to spread ink in the shape of a Y. Or why. Do
you count the days until you're burned at the
stake? I'm Avraham, the son of Avraham.
Celebrating valentine's day as I roast

Answer 1

i will not survive this winter. the
boys with fistfuls of matchsticks are

pound. pound. pounding. at
my cottage door. while

witches may be flammable, the
match-boys cannot burn the heart shape my

lover's lips take on when she whispers my
name through the dark. the

match-boys cannot burn the
mother-to-daughter tales sliding off

the angry tongues of my ancestors
for centuries to come. (they'll

inherit my flames & store them in their veins for later
& they'll have the match-boys to thank for it.)

the match-boys cannot burn the wronged
woman's wrath of artemis, goddess

of hunt(ing the boys who come for
women like me with hate-blaze eyes.) i

may not survive this winter,
but my dragonfire will last through them all.

Question 2

I'm bleeding robusta in slow-wave
sleep, burning my parchment coat
into the sand of Budapest. Dancing
eyes in my kitchen, perhaps some
jövendölés to fade young, with no
crema. Is it possible to sleep your
way to an early grave? I float upon
the Danube's silver face, searching
for the wedding ring my ancestors
lost in Hungary's tear. I find rapid
eye movement as a crippled wreck,
pure love by chance, by soul, by life.

Answer 2

the internet stranger man-boy loaded with
rehearsed bedroom eyes, arctic wolf smirks,

& dark roast breath says to me, "you're
too young to be so tired. you can sleep when

you're dead, darling." in the air above his head, i
edit his words to turn them into something i

can actually agree with, the girl loaded with a
disinterest she can't hide, three sweaters that can't

stop the shivering, & a parent-shocking secret (a
never-sterile razor taped to the bottom of her mattress).

"you can sleep when you're **wish to be**
dead, darling." *perfect.*

Question 3

I consider a pentagram on my arm
to exorcise the weight of the world
on my shoulders, pressed firmly
by the scale of my taatto's lies.
Gold threaded embellishments
weave a journey into my eighteenth
birthday. There is an arc of light
in the corner of the room, the cat
stares, I stare, knowing I'm something
close to an adult now. When does it happen?
When do we phase over into maturity
and something resembling an adult? I still
don't feel it. I was never adult enough
to hear of the noose he wanted
to put around his neck, but adult enough
to be fed those words anyway.

Answer 3

I.

as an infant
i was

                  tiny
                  pink
                  helpless
                  frog-like

& my mother
changed my diaper
with duty & precision
& i would only guess a cigarette
haphazardly sandwiched between
two of her kitchen-manicured fingers

II.

as a middle-aged woman
my mother was

                  tiny
                  grey
                  helpless
                  dead-frog-like

& hours after
changing her diaper
with *huffing* & **puffing** & wet eyes
(i watched) through the bathroom window
as nameless&faceless strangers carried (her) out
to be (burn)ed

– (& i didn't feel anything)

Question 4

Today we left the house
and managed to spend the last of this week's

wage on salad, and cat food, and orange juice.
There were too many people

in the aisles, and a vegetarian family
at the next till who clearly didn't get the memo
on Uggs. We watched the kids

run riot and attack the impulse buys
like locust to a jellybean factory.

[kinda confused and not sure how to succeed]

And we knew we were just
5 short months
away from other people watching us
watching our new born cry.

There is a smugness in living external
to experience, don't you think, Amanda? A series
of ignorances that will soon recede and die. We bought

quorn
and
products not tested on animals
and
were proud of ourselves. Because we don't wear
Uggs.

Answer 4

yes, aaron,
i guess
you could say
there's a certain
smugness
in living external
to an experience
that will
eventually
come
crashingintoyou
like an oncoming
train.
like the train i
sat stalled in
for
over an hour
& complained
incessantly
to my mother
about
being late
to the concert
while men
in protective suits
scraped pieces
of the
suicide jumper
off the tracks.
it's like
all those
years later
waking up
at half past
noon
skin-under-fingernails

angry with
myself
for
not thinking
of that
way out
first.

Question 5

Imagine me dressed as Godzilla
drunk on fine wine.
That's Saturday nights
          – that's how I waste
          my
          life.
Who sets the agen
                              da
                                        and
why?
Imagine me watching Godzilla
sipping sleepy time tea.
That's actually my nights
          – that's really how I waste
          my
          time.

Answer 5

catch me
in bed
playing
with matches
surrounded by
the letters
i never sent
the monster-boy
who shares your
name.

catch me
lighting
          blowing out
lighting
          blowing out
lighting
          b l o w i n g o u t
matches
surrounded by
the letters

i never sent
i never sent
i never sent
i never sent
i never sent

catch me
eating those
flames
next to the
sleeping
cinnamon-boy
who
couldn't save me

from him/myself/him/
                   myself.

(no one
ever
could have
& i know
he still
loves that
six years
one wife
one child-with-his-big-bad-wolf-smile
later.)

when
the smoke
wakes the
cinnamon-boy
he sits up
in bed
& eats fire
with me
& the letters
remain unharmed.

– who sets the agenda? who follows it anyway?

Question 6

I woke up,
made breakfast,
got my shit together for the day,
kissed my partner goodbye,
put my hands on our child
through a thick layer of belly,
and heard my alarm ring.

And then I woke up,
and I had dreamt it all,
and I smiled
because I knew
I could kiss her again
and feel our child kick
through that thick layer again.

I left
hoping to hear my alarm ring.

What moments do you
wish you could
relive,
dreamlike
and phantasmagorical?

Answer 6

the grey-black
      smoke
leaks from
      the cracks
of my skull
      when i try
to stir up
      a happy moment
before all
      this

      (don't take me back.)
      (don't take me back.)
      (don't take me back.)
      (don't take me back.)
      (don't take me back.)

&
the
only things
i'm left with are
the stained pages
& crooked dogears
& cold, sockless feet
& cracked summer windows
& a cat snoring at the foot of my bed
& a feeling like just waking up is an adventure.

RUPERT LOYDELL

Question 1

I am wasting away, baking under
that halogen moon
with the flowers crowing
at my feet. And the cats.
And the coats. And

perched on a floor of bacteria,
breaking my back for
a chance to catch the rain.
There are better ways to
find inspiration. There are better

ways to kill my demons
than flogging my working-class
lifestyle to within an inch of
its stereotypes. Where do you exi
st? How do you find inspiration?

Answer 1

I exist where I am,
am worn out from trying
to be otherwise.
Inspiration is a state
of mind not a moment
to aspire to. I believe
in processes and forms,
poems triggered by
overheard words
or something strange
in the news, a blue
in the corner of my eye.
I work to make words work
then use the cat to calm me
when the world gets too much.

Question 2

Laments +
Incantations
failed to resonate with me –
because I seek to understand
why the notches on bark are still
so tender, rather than to examine
the shape and call it nature.
What do you search for
in using your
words?

Answer 2

I search for awkward
-ness and surprise,
strange contrasts
and juxtapositions,
ways to re- and de-
contextualise all
the noise around us.

It's more of a filter
than a search,
there's so much
language in the air
I find it hard to
listen or to hear.

Parataxis. Collage.
Words as dodgems:
bumping and bruising
each other; atoms
spinning, invisible.
Parts put together
to make wholes.

Question 3

        and there is peace
four thousand
one hundred
odd
miles away.

        but it is sinking
into the sand
and forgetting I
ever
called it a father.

Shiring

        so I drown
with every rapid
eye movement,
para
somniac. Praying

        to be heard
four thousand
one hundred
odd
miles away.

Shearing

        How far have
you gone to
make maps
and
burn bridges?

Answer 3

Mostly, bridges
were burned
before me:
my father dying,
a friend in a car
crash, grandma
gone away.

The farthest
I've ever gone
was to here,
uprooting family
and leaving
a house I loved.

Hindsight is
a marvellous thing.

I write through
my worries,
make maps
with words
torn from
other pages,
assemble
instructions
for the future.

Foresight is
a wonderful thing.
(If only we'd
known back then.)

Question 4

Let us be writers,
in the arc of the night
meeting morning,
waiting for Prynne's first snow.
Why not any other pursuit?
Above all else I find
there is reason to calcify
all emotion
into ink
and pour it onto paper.
Let us be midwives.

Answer 4

I don't want
poetry as emotion,
it's not empathy
and ego, it's all
about language.

I don't presume
my experience
is worth more
than anyone else's,
try not to presume

at all. Midwife
to poems, perhaps;
but I have plenty
of other pursuits
to explore too:

paint and pencil,
music, boats,
real ale and
conversation.
Wait for no-one.

Question 5

Whether a blue
or a blur,
in the eye
or I,
each decision must
provoke,
or presume
that the reader
cares about the choice.

I read your beginnings
as tempted to a poetry group
by Brian Louis Pearce.
I wrote
before being welcomed,
but wrote
poorly.
It wasn't until you
burst my bubble

and helped me kill
my darlings,
that I felt I even cared
which words to use.
Do you feel you've played
that role in any other
lives? Or had that
role performed
for you?

Answer 5

Brian was a sweet man
and we were friends
until he died. He taught
me about syllabics,
modern art, how to
see with a writer's eye.

I'm sorry I burst
your bubble but
it seems to have
worked out well.
Yes, many gave
me a hard time
about my work
and made me
start again.

Andy Brown arrived
in Exeter full of avant-
garde experiment;
Tony Lopez taught
me on my MA, and
I stopped writing
for a while because
it was all so new
and my head got
in a whirl.

If they pulled me
toward experiment,
the physicality of words,
then others since
have made me look
at content again –
how to rant and rave,
at love and the lyric,
how words sit with song.

I hope I've changed
writers' lives, or
at least their writing.
I've published authors
who've gone on to
be famous, taught
student writers who
now have book deals.
I hope they have fond
memories, but it's all
their own work I read.

Question 6

I never know what words to build
into brick, wet walls, when my
trauma has healed. Where to place
punctuation, when my mouth
is void of exclamation
marks. What questions to field
when I've trimmed the bark
and triggered synthetic
sunshine from unexpected
punchlines. What ways to kill
my angels when my demons
are avenged and descend.
What good is a poet when
he has no reason to write?

Answer 6

No use at all.

But words
are always
enough reason
to keep on.

I have never
run out of
ways and means
and processes.

And trust me
I think there are
too many poets
and poems
in the world
all of no use.

That's our charm.

TEIGE MADDISON

Question 1

Amba Geshen
Amber Gershwin
Amara – bound
Mount Amara – Abyssinia
Snakes again
Against stakes
Never my DNA
DNA a stamp
Or a plant?
Heirs to a throne
Heaven never wanted
To overthrow
Be overthrown
Foul ball
Imprisoned – in prison
Prisoner as Takla
Maryam
Mirage
True cross
Krossdeath
Amba Geshen.

Answer 1

Dear Poetry,
look out of your windows
take off the latch
slide through the empty mouth
so your legs hang into the living room
and your arms curl around the window's lip.

now lean backwards into the looming
drop behind you.

know that some poems live like myth,
falling into the sea,
crashing
waves rolling on unconcernedly.

also know that others live as songs of harmony,
others mind-pits for torture, others self-aggrandising
wanks in the mirror,
others canonical pillars, others rot in desk drawers,
others never to be seen, others etcetera etcetera.

Dear Poet,
Dear Poem,
Dear Poetry,

look out of your windows,
take off the latch and slide through
the empty mouth into the looming drop below-

Have trust that your legs won't break.

Question 2

A child. Alone in their room.
A half broken music box pierces
the air with magic. A
lullaby. Christmas Eve. Anticipation.
Drums sound before a piano plays,
interrupted by heavy sounds. Motor
engines roar. Street racing. Adrenaline.
Power. A fight breaks out

between the beats. Leather jackets
drag race up and down the street.
Rebels. Got style. Got swagger. Trash
can music blares from where we, the poor
people live. Junk music performed by
dreadlocks. Cops fight crime in the
distance. A voice serenades the crowds
underneath a glorious, domed

ceiling. Rich men smoke cigars in
a boardroom. They sit back. They
relax. The child alone in its room learns
piano, a classical expression of emotion.

Two women sit hand-in-hand, side-by-side
in a hotel room. The TV is tuned to the news
but it is indecipherable. One woman turns to
her lover, moistens her lips, and says

"Kiss me." There are no moments
for the other team to shout over, no hostile
words in a setting so sweet. Just the joy
of lips vacuum packed to lips. The crowd
begins to cheer, protest banners are lit,
the world continues to turn. Magic is more

than a box of tricks in child's bedroom, don't

you think? It's the grasp of a broken
hand in a splint made from the stolen air
of a hotel room where room service forgot

the salt. Hotel rooms always smell of empty
film classes and broken camera lenses. It's
the expense forms that line the building
with sustenance, and the hearts of a thousand
lovers, torn from their homes and forced
to re-enact something close to acceptance

in a steel tube, some fifty miles below the
surface of Jupiter's third moon.

Answer 2

Questions.
A whole life is spent by answering
Questions,

I have spent my whole life answering questions.
Questions,

I have spent my whole life answering my questions.
Questions,

I have spent my whole life answering her questions.

Question.
Why am I answering this question?

Question.
You do not know?

Question 3

Why are we speaking in tongues /
why are we not splitting the atom?

You've taken a stick to the proverbial bush,
but still haven't told me who you are,
or how the snow feels on your skin,
or where you hide during thunderstorms,
or what your earliest memory of failure is.

I don't know you yet, Teige,
but I know your games.

Answer 3

Know my games:

1. I like list poems
2. I wrote this outside underneath a sycamore tree
3. I live in London
4. I once read an issue of Potato Review and I may have enjoyed it.
5. If coffee burns my throat, I may just throw it out with the computer I am writing this on
6. If I normally write in a notebook, why am I writing on a computer?
7. I eat cereal with a soup spoon
8. My name is pronounced similarly to an animal in a famous Blake poem
9. . . . .
10. Guilt. I don't like it. Gotta fill in the gaps somehow
11. .
12. [Photo of Jigsaw from the movie Saw.]
13. I hope you saw the pun in this line.
14.
15. Going to the ATM, the ghost of monies past jumps out at me from the card slot
16. 'Dude. There's no point.'
17. I hope you like games Aaron.

MAUREEN MILLER

Question 1

Have you ever disappeared?
I burnt my phone card,
        rid myself of:
                MK,
                AM,
                Japanese clothing store dismissals,
                Transatlantic screams,
                Apartments I never wanted,
                Careers I couldn't afford,
                Espressos and Ristrettos and Americano,
                rejection letters from:
                                Journals,
                                Magazines,
                                Job Interviews,
                                Universities,
                Parasomnias,
                All day forcing booze,
                Stolen sofas,
                SA80,
                TR13RA:
                                Gary at TR152ET,
                                the 1st, 2nd, 3rd affairs,
                                ceilings – dropped,
                                stairs – Pikatrapp,
                Coalition governments,
                Faslane,
                Helensburgh,
                Redruth,
                Truro,
                St Austell,
                Plymouth,
        Never home,
        Never home,
        Never home.

Answer 1
For Hannah Frank

going on as Goose was wont to do
is to be left to one's own devices

and ohh was she sent from one

      HNNH
         (uhm)

            HN,
            NH,

      WOMAN
         (ungh)

    wonking about who knows what,
    or to what effect, e.g. "tell jokes w/threes in twos,"
    plus record store dismissals, recs I never wanted,
    references I couldn't lord, Eisenstein and Akerman,
    and never heard of that man, or see more in comments

        Paltrow saying "Hoboken" over and over
again, for ~10 mins.

         hnnh?

        (unbelievable HMF)

    the things you said: all day, wordplay,
    the ganders at whose flesh was cooking
    last clauses – dropped, lost causes – copped,
    the hyperacusis for who was pandering

      and suddenly a notification:

GOOSE.
FLED.
COOP.

I was coasting and the kowtows
to you in this poem form
started you-ing in 33's
(you were, of course, punning)
in a hurry to release

I went for a dunk off the headboard
and shattered every ounce of self-respect
just embarrassing myself, goosefeathers
errywhere, all over the damn place,
looseygoosey disgracefest, never actually

      writing to this all too sudden
      vamoose of yours !

          Your X-treme vetted
          gosling go-betweens
          stomped up five stairflights
          tracking shorn plumes
          on pilgrimage to that crowded
          house of yours In Hoboken.

          Welcome home, palindrome.

          Your dream is not over.
          We've fallen,
          but you won't get up.

DANIEL OWEN

Question 1

I drew the owls from the
depths of my mind on the suitcases
strewn across the hallway
like heaven in a pack of crayons.
Is it ok to fight sometimes?
To squabble in the depth of a well
over whose line had the better resolution?

I pay attention to the throne,
the way I speak my working class
as I sing messages of martyrdom,
insomnia, desire.
So even when she screams, I know
with closed eyes she is God in third trimester.

Answer 1

It's ok to fight sometimes
even when, speaking, the
message becomes its third
point and one sees
one speaks a triangle
in the long lines of
revolutioment, searchable
and embarassed.

Question 2

…I've seen that triangle,
Daniel, have you?
I've seen it do spiteful things.
It tore me from my house
and gave me to the universe
so I could be shredded into stardust
and used as bath bombs.

Answer 2

Regretfully
the triangle's absence
amounts to the same star
that houses the triangle

when I dust I turn
my back to dust
when I wake in a square
I regret that it's not
all other squares

preferring to turn stickiness
into elasticity
I go out to the ignorant woods
and pretend to touch a leaf

Question 3

The woods, in glory and loss,
are tossed in ignorance and live
lively, lovely, always us, in stars
and constellations to confirm our
lost. I never plan on losing the road
but when I do I paint my arms
in nuclear code. Do you live safe
or safely live lost? I am wed to the idea
of a miner's life, though my county
has lost the tin and lost their way
by swinging right and choosing wrong.

Answer 3

All the woods harvested
the forrest tossed
the tin excavated
constellations lost to perfect
grids of translatable crops

I don't live except in mouse-
holes mouthing history off
watching the bananas ripen
from a far vantage – the shape of
the moderns' cruelest wishes

CYRUS PARKER

Question 1

(1)
Two miners,
an argument
about television
and us.

(2)
Heaven frozen
over. A
cartwheel over
the garden wall.

(3)
The bulk of my
memories: Glimpses
of sun amongst
burns on a triangle.

(4)
The bulk of yours,
Cyrus? A flash of
a white wall,
two school

(5)
children dancing
on the graves
of a nun
[a suicidal

(6)
father]
and a stone's
throw from
blissful boredom.

Answer 1

my memories?
a blinding
white blanket
stained with inky tendrils,
watching, waiting,

hungry
for the souls
of those
foolish enough
to test
my kindness,
graciousness.

the false prophet had to
die,
for that is the price
of knocking
on my door.

but
the boys,
oh, those boys.
they too
had a
toll
to pay.

herein lies
the difference;
the priest
demanded
my power,
yet offered no sacrifice.

the boys
sought only to
borrow
what they needed,
yet offered a sacrifice:
all for one.

Question 2

Eventually the doctors will strangle the good from my throat.
There are seventeen moths living in the back of my mouth,
masking the holes in my gums, masking the holes in my gums.
We always go back to the same coffee shop to advocate
for the symptoms of a hiatus hernia. The coffee is volcanic
in ways Nescafe would describe as 'good for young children.'
The acid reflux is worth two Americanos, and an espresso
on Sunday mornings, count the hours at night because
you'll never get them back. Premium grocery lists don't
shimmer like haikus, but every list is a series of traits I never
want to inherit. Do you read notes left on shop floors?
Scour the enemy's predictions, the stock of cat food, the rise
in cheap cereals, the Blue Danube Waltz across the
cigarette stand. Burn the doctors, burn the caffeine, burn
the groceries, it will all be ok, it will all mask the holes.

Answer 2

but isn't that human nature, though?
to find comfort in the things that destroy us,
to mask the pain with something even more hideous,
so we might feel a little less ugly
when we look at ourselves in the mirror.
so we might feel a little less ugly
when they look in from the outside.
i've lived with masks, and without,
and while hiding behind a face that isn't your own
makes it easier to get to sleep,
what lies underneath that façade
is what will haunt you in your nightmares.
i've been trying to take the mask off now and again,
to get to know the stranger that wears my face,
and i've learned how he copes:
he eats until knives carve their way out of his stomach
to fill a hunger that will never be satisfied
(the knives, they make more holes, but he knows just how to
        fill them);
he drinks until words spill out of his fingers
to fill a hole even hate dare not touch;
he fills notebooks with incomprehensible lines of poetry
because he need them to think he has his shit together more
        than he does;
he reads the notes on the shop floor
because he needs to know he has his shit together more than
        they do.
he too has moths in his throat, you see,
and he burns every single one of them
that dares leave a hole unfilled.

Question 3

Chance is Broadway Joe Nameth.
I'm off-Broadway Silas Weir Mitchell.
Two pages short of a full dictionary.
Am I ready to get spiritual?
Are you ready for your miracle?
Possibilitarian, or probabilitarian.
I can't even spell Katholic, let alone live it.
My religion is reason and my reason is Emma.
Late December blue skies & low tides.
Now that's some real mermaid.

Answer 3

i pray to my pen
because only my words
can set me free.
the seven deadly sins
serve as my "how to" guide
in living life to the fullest
because the only "god"
i answer to
is myself.

everyone could use a miracle,
but the idea
of being indebted
to some invisible entity
is enough to keep me
from shouting into the void.
i'm sure karma is waiting
to knock me down a few pegs,
anyway.

ROBERT PEAKE

Question 1

This is a line,
this is another,
this is a third,
now form a career
based upon hyperbole
and a weak [at
best] attitude to correcting
their assumptions.

Country,
BlueGrass,
Blues.
Never a writer,
always a showman [at
best]. Let John Holstrom
copy Will Eisner
in creating a road

to ruin, built on family
matters. I heard
about the
Easter Bunny,
did you? I mean,
it's a pretty
wonderful
world.

Answer 1

Yes, I heard. In the mumbling of crickets. Tell them
to make a career of chanting, and let the stars hold up
their placards, eject a weak link from the grasslands.

I pour the antidote into a blue glass of milk, carry it
down the aisle. Bystanders consider this performance art.
Draw back the veil and kiss me under the flash bulb.

I can always say I was joking, say it wasn't really me.
In these parts, they beat court jesters, don't they?
My motto: all truth, all slant, all the time.

Or your money back.

Question 2

I would catch the fly
and live homeless on promised
land, across the Pacific
Railroad.

"Perserverance as novelty"
they suggested, "hobohemia
for the ages." I'm not sure I
believe

in Kansas, two taps, but I'd
like to give it a shot. How about
you? Where is home, your
heart?

Answer 2

The mist occludes my sight most mornings.
This does not mean I dwell within a cloud.

I have hungered for the desert, returned
to find an entirely new population of sand.

If Buddha dwells in the gap between thoughts,
who fixes His roof, who stokes the stove?

I have learned to love my thoughts, even when
they turn against me. Let me fold a paper boat

for us to float on puddles until swamped.

Question 3

Rendered as a denial of service, I've been hoarding man
uscripts like I hold
evenings alone – untampered, unseen, unwanted
silence. Do you kill your

darlings? Do you let them slip the
echo, breach? I'm running

guarded for the inevitable heat death of the
universe, burning
empires and Achilles so I can be
render my heel immortal. I would
ride to Mysia, deliver my scribe,
enter anew world that does not want me

Answer 3

The wound is deep in the circuit's breach;
the wound will not go away. We dwell in it.
Flip the switch on cyber warfare in your mind.

One one side of the wound, we write, drawing
blood in which to bathe for eternal youth.
We ride on bright amniotic lightning.

The far side of the wound is darker, bruised
an orchid purple from endless worrying.
Here the drone armies whirr conspiracy.

One agency is hoarding exploits against you.
Another firewalls off your best laid plans.
You see how we tear the sutures, scratching?

The wound is buried far from algorithm's reach;
we dwell within the wound and will not go away.
Close the loop, and let the current scream.

Send out your little machines on virus limbs.
Somewhere, a host will take to the infection.
We need every kind of sickness to be healed.

Question 4

They performed a laparotomy, needed to give me
the dirt. Sixx Sixx Sixx, shouting at the devil
tearing my body apart. Peritonitis as an excuse
to ingest bass lessons, take track five from album
five before every meal. Symptoms may include
pen and paper. Treliske – to change my life. Has
your path ever altered?

Answer 4

What I thought was a path turned out to be
where the river had abandoned its landscape.

The portcullis spikes slide into well-worn places.
How dark a red leaf, evacuated of chlorophyll.

Where is my mother? Her shopping trolley abandoned.
How bright the glint of a scalpel under surgical lights.

She reminds me to keep breathing, though my lungs
give back only sea-foam, specked pink with anemones.

What I thought was the path turned out to be
just this breath, and this breath, and this.

Question 5

Floating unaided, held together by felt and glitter,
there's luminescence in my corner. Strength
in the form of a girl who doesn't care for poetry
but forgets that she is all of my descriptions
bundled up and kept in a secret pact. She is
nine tenths of the sun's warmth. A reason
to believe in Aztec Gods. A beacon for our cats
to romance her and forget I exist for anything
but food. Have you got a light when the power
cuts out? She is more than the charms, and I feel
her glow caress me when I'm weak. There are
reasons to kill demons now I've woke to
a turquoise smile.

Answer 5

"Instead of so many elegies to the dead, you should write more love poems to the living." -Marvin Bell, admonishing me

It is not the clockmaker, who keeps his own time,
in a pop-up shop next door to my pineal gland,
who reminds me with clanging bells and the insistent
clatter of gears wearing down their own teeth,

but a curl-headed mermaid, replete with shell bra
who clatters up the stairs with saucer and cup.
She looks bright in bad weather, including my own,
so lifebuoy be damned, one dry thought in a downpour

is enough to keep your head above pooling ink,
its come-hither sheen and indelible longing.
She pulls back my monk's hood, spilling daylight
on the tonsured duomo of my steam-coughing brain.

She bids the black dog heel, though it still
walks beside us. Sometimes, she tosses a stick.

Question 6

When I started these interviews,
these correspondences,
I always wrote about home
or the lack thereof.
Some gnawing doubt
that I would never find a warm bed
somewhere within a safe space.
I wrote a whole series
about St Day Road
where I grew up,
turned it into a short film.
Moved onto Richards Crescent –
which I work through at night now.
Will find myself in Mitchell Court
soon.
I think I've found home,
here in a place on the outskirts
of Truro.
In a place I don't care to live
with a girl I will always a love
and a child I will soon meet.
I guess home really is where the heart
is,
not where the luxuries exist.
So tell me, Robert,
where is home to you?

Answer 6

Home is the place I never write. When what was once familiar now feels strange, that is the strangest feeling of all. Who are these people, carrying their duke on a litter, and lions in cages to release into the chambers of the Senate? How can I look them in the eye, and say the word, "countrymen"? Home is any place our animal selves can defend. Home is a wall, when you are within it. Between wanderlust and home-longing, a soul is forged. One day the decision to exhale will be final. Meanwhile, we choose our leaders based on how much they frighten our enemies. How quick we were to judge those who could not turn back the gears of history. We forget with each new birth the necessity of kindness, bursting from our mothers' wounds, already smeared with blood. The slate is dusted clean by galactic clock-makers who see the near-collision of planets as a quaint, irresistible game. We have exhausted the gamut of possibilities. Now the tumblers fall into place within the lock. The lies that sound like common sense are painted in ever-larger letters overhead. (Since the truth is a footnote for scholars and other élites.) Let the record show: I was exiled years after I left.

CHERYL QUIMBA

Question 1

I am the board
in a maternal zero-sum game,
push net into my brothers' bank accounts.
We had no disagreement point,
no way to resolve our genes
without calling in the armed guards.

I wish it had been stochastic,
actions by nature. Do you roll the dice?
Do you call the odds
when Taleb's black swan theory
throws up double sixes.
Hail mary. Hail luck. Hail loss.

Answer 1

Remember that day
when I rounded the corner
to jump into the waiting
getaway car
and you weren't there only
candy bar wrappers
on the sidewalk a couple
dented soda cans clumps
of dead grass
I was panting kept
looking over my shoulder
ran across the street
and down the block just
in case and it was so hot
the sun rising in a perfectly
cloudless sky
it wasn't even
summer yet no kids
jumping like jelly beans
in the streets do you
remember because
that day you were not
there

Question 2

'Следите за россиян'
he told me,
pointing to a map
where all the borders had been daubed
in permanent marker,
land masses clashing five, ten, twenty miles wide.
Sure thing, but Putin didn't kick me in the chest.

He grabbed me by the lapels
in one of many hydraulic spaces
and whispered
'hætta standast'
spitting words like bullets in a knife fight. Do you know
that feeling? The torture
of a stolen voice?

With words that ushered in a new age
he said
　'太った男が小さな男の子が見たいです'
and while I caught grammatical errors
and mistakes that surely cast him
as anything but a pro,
I knew I was fracturing
like bark struck by an axe.
Sutoraiki. Sutoraiki. Sutoraiki.

Azure horses struck our ubåt
as he struck my chest.
'öppna ögonen' he pleaded,
as if causing pain is only half the fun
if you can't ride the crest
of somebody's anguished look.

I forced my fists into his stomach
and I realised that is what a real man feels like,
all gut, no guts.

'Je suis en charge'
he swore with all the grace of a matador being
speared by his favourite bull.

He almost cried
when he told me
'Io non sono il nemico'
with his hands deep in my pants,
my back leaking crimson
from the valve he forced it into
and my eye swearing vengeance
from the bruises he cast.
True, but the enemy never grabbed my cazzo.
My fasz.
My bod.

If I could've written this poem in Hungarian, Greek or Ar-
abic
I would've,
his tongue has fucked the English language.

Answer 2

Possible I misunderstood
the command as I fumbled
for my seat while others around me
stood, but it's possible too
that this day was unlike
all of the ones I had lived before,
that each word as it hit
my ear was colliding with my body
for the first time each
instant,
that my senses were in the process
of forming still, slowly
expanding as they awoke,
were born, bumped against
the contours of the room
in which we had all of us gathered,
along with all else material
and immaterial that its square
dimensions held, possible
when I heard stand I had
no recourse, could only
reel.

Question 3

That halogen moon awakens me
reminds me that these words
are all I have left and you can have them.
You can keep them.

g/h/o/s/t

tear me apart and pull out something beautiful
something necessary. Do you ever want to be
rebuilt from the ground up? I am grit after a downpour
crimson leaves in the first week of autumn.

I am lost through the night with dreams of
greater men – they
all have podium finishes, they all glow in glorious
……..colours whilst I fail.
I am /failing/
/falling/
//drifting//
///empty///

geist. In spirit (l)on(e)ly.

Restart. Begin fresh. new.
Restart.
Re****t

Answer 3

The person I was when I was reading Frankenstein
late at night, in bed, wondering
which parts of me must be monstrous
can I see them under the street light
Or listening to the market report while idling
I might never be thoroughly
good, or listening to a semi-stranger
tell me about his lower back pain, knowing
I am no longer the person I was
when I was reading Frankenstein,
No one talks about the function of the Arctic
in that story, how one creature followed another there,
how the cold was a stimulant and a balm,
how there was a man alone, on the ice,
Knowing I have days and days
that are bent, watching what could be
a fly on the baseboard or a movie about a boy
who seldom smiles, knowing I am
not the person I was when I was reading
Frankenstein, how could I be, listening to the hums
and whistles of an old-timer's bar, the counter
cracked, the stools uneven, what a comfort I am
no longer the person I was when
I was reading Frankenstein I might have been
younger then or older or made of something
else entirely I was so much half-monster
or turning more mine, reading
those nights in bed I had notions of what
cold must have felt like to a man desperate to find
that I am no longer the person.

DEAN RHETORIC

Question 1

I filled in a form to declare myself financially inept,
but not inept enough to order pizza.
The ford was run over by a white van man.
I didn't make my own coffee:
Dan did:
Twice.
We watched Good Will Hunting,
I wanted my wife to understand me better.
We watched Practical Magic,
my wife wanted to be a witch.
So we made bath bombs.
So we made more bath bombs.
The second batch worked.
Nobody wrote about the technical aspects of their exam
work.
My mentor lost her tangle teaser.
I awoke without punching the air,
so I punched the air in delight.
So I punched the air in delight.
Punched the air in delight.
Air.
Delight.
Prazosin.
Please.
Melatonin.
Please.
How was your day?

Answer 1

I awoke to a swelling paradigm between my legs
and a hopefulness,
fake as English compliments.

A childhood memory had been ignored long enough
to grow facial hair,
in my sleep this pubescent

anecdote with a beard throws stones at my frontal lobe.
My bones have been
sneaking out through an untreated

scar to play with it in the mud. They return with
less calcium on
their breath, singing **go fuck yourself**

…..(in D- Minor)

I watched an autopsy scene in reverse to see if
beautiful things could
exist inside of cold, redundant objects.

The Lambs were silenced in dissolvable packets
of insecure weather and
It rained twice before breakfast inside of me.

When this starling of apathy dies, place Moth Pupa
alarms inside this throat
to test the baritone of its infected kitchen sink.

There's no need to rush.

We have all the time in the world.

Louis Armstrong **(1901–1971).**

Question 2

In reverse an autopsy is just
yspotua na
and that's all there is to it
whether in D-Minor
or the miner
stood in the centre of the town
I grew up in
arms folded
born of the working class
fears we were all taught
to embody

Did I ever tell you how my dad
used to send me to school
telling me to tell my teachers
that Thatcher was the best thing
to ever happen to this country
and now all my school years
are tainted
with this weird
hatred I was made to embody
with a statement that feels
damp and hollow
like the stare
that evil iron lady
bore into the centre of my dad's skull

This was before
he obsessed with David Icke
and lizard people
and angles to hit towers at
and bullet holes in truck doors
and climate change denial
and all of these other conspiracies
he force fed us until we spewed it all up
in front of the class

and our educators
as if some zombie spouting
hate
and begging for anybody
to point us in the right direction

My teacher told me that sometimes
fathers need a mouthpiece
and I should research his words
and now I'm not sure who I'm angrier at
my father
or Thatcher
but I know I don't have a nice thing to say about either.

Answer 2

{illumin@ti f@ther @utopsy}

< ? P.F. Version"2.0" encoding"R.I.P._I.Q." ? >
< ! – – HP Search V2 30+1+1 http://www.hereditaryblack-eyeview.com – – >

<report>

<footage summary>

{a birth//a kidney bean with eyes//a sack of flour with a heartbeat}
{a death//a house//a body//looks content//when no one is inside}
{a child – an interruption – forever}

<file size **O** -01- In this American remake of his sleep
<file size **U** -02- paranoia leaves a basket at the front door
<file size **T** -03- a baby hurricane, cooing softly inside,

<file size **C** -04- a weaponised love song – fragile – irresponsibly held.
<file size **O** -05- Attached to the basket is a note: You were screaming
<file size **M** -06- and scratching through dreams again, grinding your
<file size **E** -07- lungs against the bedpost. Please find enclosed your

<file size **T** -08- carbon dioxide lovechild. [MONTAGE]:
<file size **H**-09- He falls asleep on a train and the baby starts to
<file size **E**-10- scream, limbs spinning wildly throughout the carriage.

<file size **B** -11- Have you ever seen an unpredictable infant of weather
<file size **O** -12- phenomenon shitting its pants? Begging to be changed,
<file size **N** -13- under the crippling migraine of minimum wage studio lights?
<file size **E** -14- Masculinity is a frightened child's diagram of a throat
<file size **S** -15- pretending to be a map of the universe.

i have died in worse places than this I have died in worse places than this I have died in worse places than this i have died in worse places than this i have died in worse places

<installation – complete – copy diagram at own risk>

Question 3

Your file is corrupt Dean,
and I've eaten the core
of your heart
and found each broken
kiss to be a storm
cloud
wearing a raincoat.

September will bring
more sun
than every lung
you have kept
in your cupboard
so you can steal
the breaths
of everybody
who has stolen yours.

How do you build
hurricanes
in the centre of
your eyes?
Take a needle
and pierce the velvet
lining
of your own interior.

Buy my soul
a drink
and treat it to a meal
so I can feel special
on the day
I wear
my funeral
casket.

Answer 3

When navigating through the hurricane of your own
respiratory system, simply imagine a miniature clown
car speeding downhill with fifty five versions of

yourself suffocating inside – one of you steers along the
constantly expanding and retracting ridges of a pot
holed diaphragm whilst the other fifty four of you kick

the back of your seat, screaming childhood nicknames.
One of them covers your eyes, laughing manically. The
car spins. You punch the horn but spiders explode from

inside the wheel, gulping down the eyeball fluid out of
your screaming passengers. The upholstery of the car
shakes violently – rats crawl out from the stitching,

vomiting thick, black tar over the eyeball drinking spiders.
You approach a flashing carousel. Each horse has somebody
you love tied to the saddle. The radio flickers on – there's

a song you just can't get out of your head that goes,
'Everyone you love is dead! Everyone you love is dead!'
Your foot hits the brake only to find a note that says,

*'Are you currently working? Do you usually pay for
your motion inhibitor?'* It's too late. You're going to
hit the carousel. You turn your head and brace for impact.

Rats, spiders, broken horses, rejection emails, neon lights
and severed limbs dance to the audio bruise of your engine
music. Turn left. You have now reached your destination.

I don't know if they make a raincoat deep enough to keep those
kind of parts dry. Then again, we're all fucked, and a casket is
probably the most effective form of contraception I'll ever try.

ELIZABETH SCANLON

Question 1

When I dove two hundred odd meters
below sea level
I found creatures that both should and shouldn't
exist,
and I knew we should stop playing God.
Stop categorising
mother nature as if a library book on how to
read unicorn
dreams, or pull the fantasies from old skulls.

I threw myself head first into nuclear
remedies
and waited for the fall out to firm out,
pull me back
to that old tin mine town where all my dreams
could go to die
like my fathers and his fathers and his fathers
before him.
Where do your dreams go to die? Or get resus

citated? The road lead to my wife, and our
daughter, and
too much ER too close to the due date.

Answer 1

Everything in your dream is you,
in the Jungian mode, so you learn
to say, if say, you dream of a lion eating a turkey club,
the lion part of me is eating the turkey part of me club part of me,
to crack the code of the sleeping brain.
The lion-me wakes hungry every day and wants
to run back to the savannah to loll in tall grass.
The turkey talks jive. But the club part of me, oh the club –
it will beat you with the longing to belong.
The dream is to wake before dying.
You are not you, I am not only I, not even
in my dreams.

Question 2

The clouds are in the cornfields today
and I'm still counting the letters I receive
every time I dream of my mother. There
are always submarines, shades of regret,
and artificial sand, and me climbing into
the litter box to escape the claustrophobia.
I am not sure I am worth an award. Do you
ever celebrate yourself? Sing your own body
electric? I am still awake and still asleep
and now I have read the words pasted to the
walls, and they tell me my father will phone
today, but only to tell me it was an accident.

Answer 2

Most celebrations make me a little uneasy –
weddings, graduations, the occasional bris –
each seem to hold the promise of some affiliation
I'm not sure I can fulfill, a reckoning
of worth that makes all the to-do called for,
and/or come with a big bar bill. Though I do
like to throw a party, especially the inviting part,
the part where you say come on,
come through, there's going to be a dance-off,
a piñata, some recklessness, some ridiculousness
and it won't be any fun without you. I like to host.
Is that the opposite of self-aggrandizement, or its pinnacle?

ERIC SIGLER

Question 1
'De Stella nova in pede Serpentarii'

She turned the brightness up for fourty weeks
like a Kepler Supernova multiplied by thirteen
and a bit – rough math. Waiting impatiently for
a new star to arrive, a future for some broken
vase. She was the superglue to put me back
together, the broken parts wound tight in her
womb. I am prepared to be great. In what ways
do you find reasons to kill demons? To find glory?

Answer 1

I stood before the motion of the skies
waited for the sun to wash the stars
from every memory the moments whispered.
Had I not been there once- before all eyes
had seen what others saw- the death of Mars-
the earth he flattened rounded, edges curved,
and Kepler's 'Star' now in the pantheon,
washed up on the shores of Galilee,
giving birth to faith, to light the blind….
New hope would be the essence of ambition
to cast the tides of war into the sea,
and fish into the nets of Cosmic Mind
the parody of peace, the trust of love,
the intimations outward and within,
that some bright star will follow what we see,
that even as we answer, as we move,
we find the outer spaces of emotion-
the human element that's forged in fire-
the star that stokes this godless funeral pyre.

Question 2

I spent yesterday staring at sand and waiting
waiting waiting
waiting
for it to fill the bottom half
so I could stop talking

and start listening
listening listening
listening
to the other people begging for gold
to wrap around the broken

parts of their fragile
fragile fragile
fragile
memories where indecision has blurred
the lines between family

and all the reasons I still pikatrapp
pikatrapp pikatrapp
pikatrapp
and one day I will talk abut
the stairs, and one day I will break

tradition and not use cheap tricks
tricks tricks
tricks
to avoid the way my head still caves in. Do you understand
Eric? Do you know how to get out

of that repetition?

Answer 2

Nirvana

I spent this morning
        staring at the sea-
rolling, roiling, breaking,
while mermaids sang to me,
and in their chanting voices
                oscillations
lifted me like feathers
           lift the wind,
and minions of sea horses
           rode like stallions-
under, over, water-
              in waves that have no end…

I spent this morning
           staring at the sun,
lighting lightning flashing
through all that I have done,
        through all the sadnesses
              I have become-
a mermaid or a feather,
         a sea horse on the wind-
and as the hour passes,
        I'm derelict of sum,
a vapor in the aether,
sighing 'singing words' that have no end

Question 3

The halogen moon has taught me
to place my tears into two categories:
category A: Wasted Fluid.
category B: Best Occasions.
I've wasted most tears when I manage
to confuse the scent of discarded cigarettes
with a general yearning for acceptance.

I know it's tough, but how tough?

once I had an idea of fate, but I replaced it with
a glowing aura of decisions and consequence. I
managed to embrace the night fundamentally,
and the need for magnetic instances.
all I have left is to imagine
being five again, enamoured in situations where
I could climb a tree or build a fort. Now all my trees
are pruned and all my forts are mortgaged.

exit signs glow much in the same way the moon heralds
an intention to sleep,.
I never take the incentive.
I never take the incentive.
I never take incentives.

Answer 3

Significant of ease,
            I taste a leaf of grass-
atop the tree-topped trees
        the easy breezes dance-
                and bend-
upon my knees- to west and east.
        The sundial on the compass
                rotates by degrees,
                and then suspends

in atmospheres that hear
                the hum of light
buzzing in the ear-
        the sum of stars tonight....
                One seldom sees
a moon as large and clear-
                an infinitely bright
                sunlit candlelight
        held in the hands of the Hesperides....

There is a silver river
        that tumbles through the stars,
a sea of light that shivers
                Venus into Mars,
                and Love-
        Alive!- to constellate 'The Lovers'-
                as they are as they are-
                Halogens and Phosphors,
                        in a crystal jar...

LAVINIA SINGER

Question 1
'De Stella nova in pede Serpentarii'

Ours is not the result of Theia
nor the comparison between
a closed fist on one side of a
map and two natural satellites
hovering over Orwell's Japan.

Young's old Gods are ever-
present on Rhea, plotting to
manipulate Titan, and we wait
on train times, hand held on
a journey to fling my stem cells

across the Atlantic to a shadow
dancing in the heart of Texas.
Our sacrifice is simple, give
birth to an animal or give birth
to ourselves. And all we want

are crows, the size of houses.
Where do we mark our mass
on a map? A cross to show we
were here, or some work to
leave a voice on a grave? I

swore we saw Chiron, once,
in the cancer-tinted corner of
a streetlight. We kept it quiet,
gave Goldschmidt his victory.

Answer 1
FIRST QUARTER
Monday 3 April 2017, 19.39

astrophobia

I recognise the symptoms

lex parsimoniae

Left | right……..Set | rise

entrevoir

At first sight: could we be mistaken?

Aaru

(a kind of paradise)

Question 2

Angels the size of houses cannot hide
       from widowed giants
              behind the opium of
                     onopordum acanthium.

With hammers and mallets and whales,
       there are excuses
              to shatter the crown
                   of Cornish kings.

Have you bitten into the wrath and warfare
       of gently sewn duvets?
              Lain in molten grass
                   amongst a jury of dead roses?

In comatose sleep and glorious daydream
       the world still pivots
              on a gentle axis
                   while fairytales burn.

Answer 2
[Full Moon
Wednesday 10 May 2017, 22.42]

Skin on the ash tree
Fur in the wound
Light shifts red
The dart hits true

No house but heaven
Not bit but swallowed
Not gentle but shocked
No sleep but slain

Question 3

I've buried heaven
in your house.
Can you find it
amongst the webs?

I've lost my watch
near the river,
I hope it eventually
reaches the ocean.

I've grown old and broken
on my front porch
and read poetry
to demonic woodlice.

I've made vegetarian
fry-ups for my wife
and given ten percent
to our future.

Answer 3
[Third quarter
Saturday 17 June 2017, 12.32]

I found it hanging, flared,
a hearing trumpet angled from the heavens.
Spineless white.

Like the bullet ant
or the dream root from the river
(divine within)

it is more than ornament.
For unruly children and buried wives,
one week given to grow.

Pressed, chewed – so sweet!
But to eat this hollow food is to leave
all hope for home.

Question 4

I don't hear trumpets
when the reckoning comes,
just the silent, soft sound
of footsteps.

We all need more than one week
to grow, more time to shield
our remains from the soil
and bury our aging bones.

Where will you be buried?
In the return of graceless dancers
I will find myself torn
from their aching kneecaps,

spread wildly across
the bugle player's path
and cleaning the mess
from an unsanctioned riot.

Answer 4
[New Moon]
Sunday 23 July 2017, 10.45

It began so quietly and darkly ~~only~~ a softness to the shadow
that soothed, not menaced. ~~And here~~ I was ~~here~~ lulled into
the talk, ~~and~~ opening an ~~the~~ eye to the ~~inner histories~~ and
layered ~~desires~~ histories ~~I'd been~~ balancing in the heart. Soft
and dark, ~~you inveigling We can only hope for earthshine~~ at
a time of absent of earthshine and so inveigled, I sang and
~~spread slipped~~ the message ~~as as~~ sure as wildfire ~~but black~~
here it ~~flows, crisp light fingernail tearing the open the from
first to and last dark and how does it appear~~ slips ~~slipped~~
like a fingernail's ~~ragging raging~~ the dark, and how ~~does~~ it
has appeared ~~I can only~~ this ragged graceless path – from
first to, against the dark, last. an ~~at it is a graceless~~ account.
an unspeakable I would think it unspeakable

JON STONE

Question 1

The mausoleum is full of broken brooches,
rusted pins, and enlightened bulbs –
quiet mischief hums the tune
of saints marching in.

A child withers away in the corner,
wrinkled with crow's feet pressed
into the sides of fresh eyes.
They say the fairies

play pranks with hourglasses.
How will you attempt
to turn the sands
back once more?

In foreign languages, spoken to domestic
ears we hear dreams repeated
for eternity. In sleep age
knows only daybreak.

Answer 1

I'll tell you how, but first, hear that? The guard's asleep.
He's churring like a pylon, and that sparkling laugh?
I'd say that that's the keys he gathers at his hip.
I wonder if the murmuring's what did the trick,
what wormed beneath the door and switched the searchlights off.
Though yours and mine alone would never be enough,
there's all these cells around us, always filling up
with what I like to call that sweet electric tick.
The double sense of 'boring' comes to mind. The erk
of undercover stitching or the whirr of surf.
But I'm just mouthing rumours. Here's our sleepy prince.
The question now is how to reach those sliver-flints
that sit there at his belt, beyond our fingertips –
how to hook them, slip them in and make them speak.

Question 2

Silence, that's the way we scream when tied
heels up, neck down blood seeping through
a pinprick. Your sleepy prince is my insomniac
knight, wading through the carpeted calm and
the lunar decided misery.

What purpose do these calculated guesses have?
We believe it is three days a month, because
we don't count the other twenty eight. Those
silver-flints, they are yours to take, not mine,
I want the photo of apostasy.

Answer 2

I didn't catch the last few words there, owing to
the detonation carrying us off our feet
and tumbling us like jacks for maybe half a mile.
So just give me a moment to adjust my set.
Is this an amphitheatre or a carousel
I'm stumbling through the middle of? Don't answer that –
in fact, if you could keep it to a whisper, ta.
The way to find one's bearings in an aftermath
is through the things the hardly-noticed things reveal;
you have to play detective, spy and saboteur
in tandem, test the tensile strength of every breath –
which is the answer, I would just point out, to what
you asked back there, since after all, we bagatelle
from aftermath to aftermath, from mouth to mouth.

Question 3

It's the depth charges, Jon,
the underwater butterflies
that turn nuclear when fed
to the undercurrents.

This is a carousel in an
amphitheatre in an amphibian's
beating heart, and you're
the spawn we nurtured.

We've kept things whispered,
so far, don't you think?
Kept our voices at a level
lower than that of the dusk.

I am Auster's detective
searching for Kent who
has helped Kent team
up with a guy called Auster.

We are the spy and the
saboteur, and we are trying
to keep thing Guðless
from the Eyðileggingomb.

Answer 3

Apologies for being out of town of late,
the town in question being [gestures to his mind].
I was in exile, struck off as a reprobate,
and only gained re-entry when the gates weren't manned.
I hoped, of course, to find the place a dire state,
the law books full of damned fool statutes to amend,
the streets aghast with rubbish and inanimate,
but no such luck. Things hummed. My absence went unmourned.
I took another name and job. I manned the gate
and listened for your whispers. Being thus marooned
inside myself, however, all the inchoate
and half-said things unpick me – all the me I've mained
gets snarled up with the not-me, and I wait. I wait
for this, for that, a card, the dark, my cue, my end.

ROSS SUTHERLAND

Question 1

I'm always on standby, little red
light. Trying for weeks to telecine the remnants
of a timecode I lodged on tape somewhere between
Redruth and Glasgow. Somewhere between
here and there, climbing back up colour
bars – I swear it was after "create your own
narrative" but before "Prynne's first snow."
My mind is analogue, coated in iron
and leftover steel wire. High fidelity is for winners,
the lucky ones. How do you navigate the maze
between memory and paper?

Answer 1

Poetry is failure, that's how it finds me.
That's how I like it. A poet sets off
looking for the exit, accidentally drowns in the fountain.
Accidentally ends up in the wrong bathroom, apologising.
Accidentally knocks a kid down an open lift-shaft.

There's a conference in the rose ballroom:
7th EAST AND SOUTHEAST ASIAN
WILD ANIMAL RESCUE NETWORK.
The theme is "Perspectives, methodologies
and challenges in the reintroduction of wildlife"
The poet just takes a seat in the back
and pretends this is where they were headed all along.

Whenever I read a poem,
I invisibly add an extra line at the end:
or something like that anyway fuck this.
The empty space at the bottom of the page
is awkward silence & should be performed as such.

I take the stairs three at a time,
desperate to tell you something.
By the time I reach you, I'm too knackered to say anything of value.
(I smoke and I have asthma. Plus I have nothing to say of value).

Choose a bar at random, ask the drunkest man there
what to do next. The question makes sense,
the answer does not. At least, not yet.
I'm just trying to get away from myself, hence this
hotel in Cambodia.

Question 2

If somebody listens in, somebody booking
or scripting, I've always seen myself
as a face. There's a beauty
in creating your own downfall and calling it
Montreal,
calling it Sharpshooter, calling it
treachery. Expectations
are Heartbreak, Kid,
somebody has to blunt their bones
watching the clock turn heel.
[your career is what happens when you

write the first draft of you notice].
You can wrestle with your shadows
in the projection room, in the dead of night. Nobody
cares about the ladders, or the steel
diamonds [interlocked cage] – they only recall
the stab in the back
and the hours spent counting cat's eyes
for fifty miles, and the possibility that this all,
every second of it, might be your own
creation –
and the whole damn thing might be fake.
What do you
want to be remembered for?

Answer 2

This month I'm mostly trapped on trains

and though the British countryside is pretty in a plain kind of way
I can barely think straight with all the heat and noise.

I want to try and start somewhere honest,
Poetry makes it all too easy to duck questions.

Particularly important ones;
hence crappy love poetry, etc.

Q: Do you love me?
Poet: Hey, look at this bowl of vegetables in October.

I'm not above this shit but sometimes you just have to say,
No, I don't love you. Sorry. It's not just because of Halloween.

My self-worth is wrapped up in my writing
I can't lie and say I don't care what happens to it.

I lost a hard-drive full of poetry two years ago
and the Russian tech guy who looked at it

told me about his past life as an anarchist
and how he once put a pipe bomb

through the window of a parked car.
I walked home along the Cam river feeling

like I'd wasted all my sadness on inflammable objects.
I couldn't rewrite those lost poems.

There's something perverse
about trying to repeat those journeys.

Nothing feels as good as a spontaneous change of direction
But it's joyless to simulate such things.

Something needs to survive
But I don't think its the words.

What needs to be passed on
are the tools of poetry. The ability

to look at the queue in the passport office
and suddenly be having sex with a corpse.

(Let me try and put this another way)

What I want is the feeling of being over-written
just as I have overwritten others.

(And I know this will sound like a contradiction
based on the things I've just been talking about, but-)

I don't think you can truly understand a poem
until you've plagiarised it.

Until you have systematically removed someone else's words
and replaced them with your own.

It's like secretly moving in with your girlfriend
by bringing over one of your DVDs every night.

I know it's easier to make this claim
when your art-form exists entirely outside the flow of capital

but I think that worthlessness
is actually its greatest gift.

If you are reading poetry and not copying it I don't know
I just think that something remains incomplete.

My girlfriend's house is a different shape to mine.
Now I walk into walls where doors should be,

particularly in the middle of the night
when I'm trying to find the right room to pee in.

Time flows differently these days.
I wake up and look at her stupid blue bookcases

And don't know who the fuck I am.
But not in a bad way at all.

We're all victims of architecture, more or less.
So shout-out to every eighteen year old

typing a sort-of Bukowski poem
into his phone in the corner of a nightclub

I like the frequency with which you hit enter, kid!
Now go back to the dancefloor & sing along to Sex Bomb .

It doesn't matter, in fact it's preferable
if the only words you know are "Sex Bomb"

& as long as you keep moving
you can call it a career.

Question 3

My car is on its way to blowing up,
or falling apart –
I know this because I can feel it,
the way you can sometimes feel it's about to rain
even though the clouds aren't yet so full of themselves
they can be heard laughing while we sleep.
I drive through my hometown every single night
and wonder what I did to be lucky enough
to escape the attempted
murders and all the restlessness
[all my friends are enemies are wasted
are wasting away].
I read somewhere about a driver who died
after being struck by a loose brick, so now
I know
I won't sleep tonight. I'll be wrapped in cotton,
stuffing sand into my ears hoping those words see fit
to stay on the page. And I hope there was no passenger
to see the final moment, to watch that brick swing coincidence
into the way of
bad luck. I can hear the impact, and either silence or screams
[I'm not really sure what's worse].
You ever get that way, Ross? You ever
delve too far into the story and find yourself struggling
on the wrong side of the lifeguard flags?
Between my car and their car, I'm not really sure
I want to drive home tonight.
But I can't stay here.

Answer 3

I'm in the window of a cafe in Peterborough.
My first day off in three weeks. There's some kids
in long sleeved black hoodies despite the heat.
Old guy in aviators, scuffed Rolex. A baby
with a cyan hair-clip. A saxophone plays
Chris de Burgh I think. A man that looks like
Louis CK in a blue anorak slowly sets up
a stall in the courtyard. The sign says ENERGY
RECRUITMENT ROADSHOW. He loads
mysterious silver parcels onto a fold-out table.

This is a town of terrible dressers.
It's not just the shape of the people.

It's almost as if the city is built
on some kind of electromagnetic anomaly
that glitches out our ability to match top to bottom.
It gives the streets a kind of off-key music
Not like some awful art-rock band but nevertheless
a music that you cant talk over at the bar.

And I want to talk about other things
but christ it's distracting.

We're always half dreaming
And I try to remind myself of this.

I spend a lot of time having private conversations with the past
A kind of anti-sleep
where I endlessly accuse old friends of changing the rules.

Thats me in the grip of your car-crashes Aaron
some right hemisphere demon
Stuck in a living poem
that thinks God rhymes with the address of some ex-girlfriend.

Last week I ran away from the press night of my new play
I just couldn't take it.
It was like a dream that had escaped me.

(Old Mitch Herburg joke:
instead of following your dreams,
why not find out where your dreams are going
and then just meet up with them later.)

Instead I got a train back to Peterborough.
A bonfire went past my window
like a fireball.

And I started to wonder
if the longest creative project of my life
would be the story of How I Gave Up On Art.

God knows what draft I'm on already.

Eventually released (limited edition of one)
for friends to flip through when they shit in my house.

hugs Freddy Krueger

wakes up

Well you know what I'm talking about here.

Which is why it's good sometimes
just to just sit in the window
and catalogue the uneven fashions
of your new home town.

It feels good to translate everything
into the cold calm prose of car manuals.

Great moons of Scotland,
It's awesome to be boring
at 4:35 on the 24th of September.

Question 4

'Si deve suonare tutto questo pezzo delicatissimamente e senza sordino'

It was winter
[blue]
when they split the bark and married it
with chemicals. I was bound. Molten salts.
Press Johannes Gutenberg's words
onto the population – every byproduct of some father's
racism.
There are 290 boxes to think outside of,
to play both summer and winter
[red and blue]
for 14 times, 14 midnights, 14 full moons.

Some impromptu fantasy, I suppose.
I still call my father's name in my sleep,
in triple p dynamic, so I don't disturb the neighbours
and give them reason to care.
I like the nonchalance. Don't you?
Isn't it nice knowing you can call the cat in it at night
without worrying that next door might offer a hand?
I hallucinate, spring
[yellow]
out of bed when grass is luminescent

in twilight. Pavor Nocturnus.
Killing either God, or my father
twenty years too late for it to make a difference.
[I've already used this sentiment in a poem,
but I get lazy,
and I can't kill my demons in one stream of thought]
Buy me delta sleep, rip the turpentine and soap
from my glands. Give me beautiful sleep architecture,
house my dreams in autumn
[brown].

Answer 4

So I just phone-googled your epigraph

plus some other sections of the poem you sent
Perhaps unnecessary but it's 10pm

in a pub full of Islington haircuts
screaming at the pay-per-view boxing

so I don't know.
I don't have much faith in ignorance tonight.

Your poem had a sadness
a ghost house in dramamine

and I don't want to steer away from it.
It'd be all too easy to do so.

Poets write "responses" all the time
though they tend to fail the basic rules of conversation.

It's more like two drunks in an airport bar: "Johannes Gutenberg?
Sounds a lot like my youngest son, let me tell you—"

When we started, I told you I used writing to escape.
But the ethics feel different when you're not on your own.

It's douchey to leave a date
through the bathroom window.

And this is a date of sorts Aaron.
I'm sorry.

(Poetry is a failing restaurant
with a suspiciously broad buffet)

On my first day teaching poetry in prison
my boss led me across an empty ochre courtyard,

through endless gates and checkpoints,
the wind incomprehensible.

One, she said, never to talk about yourself.
Your students will find ways to use it against you.

Two: don't let them tell you their crimes.
Once you know, you can never go back.

I thought to myself: well this is fucking daft.
Are we just going to write haiku about dogs?

My workshops felt like waiting rooms
rap videos censored to an empty blue screen.

But over time, language began to expand
to fill the gap between us:

A torched land rover, the shadow of a mountain
A horse through a keyhole, a black kite, a nail.

Metaphor was a third place, a safe-house
we could share. A way to talk without actually talking.

But prisons are already giant code machines.
Dense with secret languages, controlled and meticulous.

An inmate needs to know the purpose of a metaphor.
Too much is at stake to leave an image in the wind.

Perhaps this is why all the cons quit the workshop.
Either we all escape together, or no one escapes at all.

Knowing full well that I can't walk through walls,
it still helps me to think of your poem as a prison.

I want to come work in it a while,
even if all I do

is collect the excuses of your inmates
as they drop out one by one

returning to some distant part of the facility
where I cannot follow, cannot even imagine.

***

'Si deve suonare tutto questo pezzo
delicatissimamente e senza sordino'

"This whole piece ought to be played
with the utmost delicacy and without dampers"

A request lifted from the opening page
of Beethoven's Sonata 14.

Is this a plea for a delicate reading,
a delicate interpretation, or a delicate response?

Should I skip though it lightly, the colour wheel spinning
the scenes into one clip of moonlight?

Or should I move slow and cautious, weigh every word,
Listen for the story behind your dream?

If I ignore someone's scar, does that make me delicate?
Or is the delicate reading to ask from where it came?

Modern players of the Moonlight Sonata
ignore this request. The piano has changed.

Now a note left undampened outstays its welcome.
(This is what Wikipedia says anyway)

The maestro's advice now ruins the song
No, don't say ruins. Say "updates".

The moon we once sought — destroyed by reflection.
Dopplered by its own waves.

I bought it on iTunes. I'm playing it now:
Steve Anderson: Classics for the Heart.

Kings Cross, empty at this time of night
glows like a kind of caffeinated heaven.

As if the dead were more awake
than any of us.

Vague shadows of the evening, pub dregs and night-shift
filtered through the snow of Sonata 14.

Unheard— but calculated by breath and moment.
As Ludwig wrote it: invisible sadness.

The last drunks, minds like pranked campus fountains
explain themselves over and over.

On a long enough timeline, we all share a past.
(The last train out of this station is mine.)

There are twelve full moons in a single year.
Thirteen sometimes. But never fourteen.

Nor do I get the line about 290 boxes.
Google just brings up storage solutions,

the 290 bus route to Twickenham…
The University of Illinois Psychology Department

has a form called 290,
but you have to log into the system to read it.

(Insert: one week later, 290 is the number
of votes that wins Donald Trump the US election.

I re-read your phrase "impromptu fantasy"
with newfound horror when I woke this morning.

I am trapped outside the dream.
I do not understand. I may never understand.

Am I asleep or awake?
Christ I want to fucking vomit)

The last train smells of terrible sleep.

I'm far too tired to keep writing
but way too far from home to stop.

A voice says Stevenage like anything matters
Outside, nothing but parallel carriages.

Release 290 on Project Gutenberg
is The Stark Munro Letters by Arthur Conan Doyle

who (based on this low res painting) was the spit of my granddad:
very much a locked room mystery of his own.

I am streaming the audio file
His robot voice carrying me back towards the fens.

The words slowly phasing into music
rocks in a fast-flowing stream.

Ghostly shapes in the darkness,
rolling over fields like black plastic.

***

Sometimes I am sent to teach soldiers.

There is a house in the country where they all live together,
different parts of them missing.

I wait in a classroom.
Some days no one comes.

My first day I asked if we could "go round the circle,
say your name and a word that you like…."

"My name is Brian. I like the word *silence*"
"My name is Rob. My word is *nothing*."

"My name is Karen. My word is *quiet*."
"My name is Christopher. I like the word *no*"

"Triple p dynamic" means pian-iss-issimo
More musical notation: play very very soft.

These days we just sit and talk about movies.
I don't care. For me, sitting down is enough.

Pavor Nocturnus — a name for night terrors.
Distinguished from nightmares, says the NCBI,

as terrors can cross from REM into deep sleep.
They follow you into the abyss.

You cry out in pain but you don't remember.
You're woken by screams, a soldier once told me,

Yet you can never tell if the noise came from you
or from a guy in some other room.

Dude, I told him, as I packed up my things.
You should definitely put that image in a poem.

My name is Ross. My word is oh fuck off.
These days I try not to scroll back up.

Each page a spent nicotine patch.
Something dead long before you arrive.

I've made my peace with things like that.

Though I still like to go to back-room bars
and listen to kids who talk like fire

who reticulate their verses
as a kind of skeezy spellcasting.

But afterwards in the pub across the road
Pay-per-view boxing on every wall

A white kid yells *my n****r* at the screen
and then nothing.

The fight continues on-screen
but my neighbours are undisturbed.

We all go to our bed every night
having failed a secret test.

Your top three Bond films,
ranked worst to best?

Live and Let Die, Casino Royale,
Dr No: that's me.

GEORGE SZIRTES

Question 1

When I see him, he is no longer clad
in his national song, no longer
crossing the Danube in confusion –
fight or flee. He is now a one-man brewery
flush with reasons. The story reminds me

of how he fled to Austria, shipped up
in Plymouth, learnt English
from Laurel and Hardy, watched my father
burn his bridges. My dictator lead

the charge against my Magyar
hero, threw sixty years of history into a broken
flat in Fraddon. They slipped through the cracks
in my father's lies, my nagyapa left
to watch the foam settle on gold

coins, silver too, as his purpose
became lost. Have you surrendered more
than you thought you could? I gave up
my family for a piece of Hungarian history, threw
away a cult for a hero.

Answer 1

The country you leave is the country you lose
The journey you take is the path that you choose.
The blue sky is blue but it's also the blues
There is no returning.

The border you cross is the border you've crossed
The language you speak is the language you lost
The footprints you make are merely embossed
They've gone by the morning.

The place where you settle is what you become
The more that you speak the more you are dumb.
The more your heart beats the more it's a drum.
The more it's in mourning.

The country is closing, its doors are now locked
The goods you once purchased are no longer stocked.
You're somebody else but no one is shocked
It's all in the learning.

You could have sung laughter, the note's on the score.
You could have loved better, you could have loved more.
You could have relaxed on the sand on the shore
Where all suns are burning.

But sometimes you leave since there's nothing to lose.
You might not have chosen but still opt to choose.
The blues are the blues are the blues are the blues
And there's no returning.

Question 2

There was a traffic cone scrawled in Magyar / I ate it / burnt the gloss from a secular refrain / where all the broken rivers / collided into a waterfall / a sonic boom / they shut down / the cupcake shop in a wonderful way / threw the flour into the streets and the chocolate icing / into a bin out the back / near the cathedral / I stood under a sign / for M&Ms where he could see me / as he stepped off the bus / my heart swelled and became a hot air balloon / we could ride over the Danube / across the channel / past St Day Road / to a place I could belong / maybe / if I could just learn to sing.

How do you learn / to make your words / sing?

Answer 2

We could ride over the Danube / or sit on the step with Attila József / watching melon-rind drift down the tide / in a summer that is intolerable / while the city is half-asleep or sheltering by Lake Balaton / near the railway track at Balatonszárszó where József / died / it is a long way from there to the city / which is a long way from here / to whatever music is sung in its tunnels / by the dead who must live there / but rarely appear on the platform / we enter through the doors of the Metro / where the nearest waterfall is an escalator descending / the other rising / in the throat / into the light of midday / where a hot-air ballon is turning to metaphor / to a heart / to a cavity / to exhaustion / to coffee / to the rococo pastry of the lungs.

Question 3

The blood fjord does not represent
the Volga river, nor does the Carn loom heavy
over the town like the Ural mountains.

I am first name then last name, born into a lie
about a messiah on the streets
of Bristol. I want to lose my genes

in Lake Héviz – blister the brown from my iris
and strip away the layers to find blue,
find my way to someone else.

Do you dream of being anybody but
you, George? I dream of being
anybody but my father

yet I still see his ears and eyes when
I look in the mirror. I shave my head and trim
my beard to avoid the best of him.

Answer 3

The river has a delta and the bodies
float down it to the sea. Many have seen them
time and again pass the Iron Gates

and drift right through Romania. It was hot.
They were unnamed and unidentified,
marking the river's course with trails of blood.

Fish followed them. The local bargemen poked
some bodies to the shore. Others were caught
in the reeds. I was watching for my father

who wasn't among them though his washed-out face
reminded me of them, transformed in dreams,
becoming an image of himself. How far

had we got in conversation? Should I remove
my false beard and trim my nose a little
to please the tales of dead men yet to come?

Question 4

Dead men do not sport false beards
under shallow graves, when the birds
rob them of their Earth. I know this
like I know my Grandfather's touch

pressed against a cold glass of beer at
four in the morning. He'd blame it on
Hungary, the booze, it was just the way
his culture demands he relax. But I still

blame it on the son-in-law who stole
his daughter and gave her away to the
broken red fjord. Do you blame your
culture for any of your flaws? Or do you

revel in the loss of instinct? I could bare
my claws and sharpen my teeth for my
father, a man who holds culture like he
holds other women. Loose and with a

wandering eye.

Answer 4

Loose and equipped with dark-brown wandering eyes,
My father imagined himself otherwise
Than I can now that he is six years dead,
His one moustache attached to one bare head.

Of course his life was darker and was shaped
By claws and graves that somehow he escaped.
Was almost dead, his fate as good as sealed
When he took off and sprinted down a field.

He wore his trilby so. He never drank
More than he could hold or safely bank.
He was a sober man of serious intent
And what was not real I've had to invent.

To know is knowing that you do not know,
That stories are built on stories you let go,
Let slip the wandering deep dark-brown eyes.
Let them all go. Let go. Stories are lies.

Question 5

You and I, George, seem to always return
to Buda, to Pest, to our fathers and the shape of their pasts.
Either the recreation of men we create stories for,
or the loss of them in lives
we lead without their input.

Mine still burns my eyelids
and causes the crow on my right hand to squawk sweet nothings
of trauma and tertiary colours into my sleeping ears.
I swallowed sleeping tablets for the last week,
and all I got was a memory of a suicide attempt
when I was 13.

I wanted to fling myself from a balcony
in a British-colonised tourist trap in Spain.
I told my djömoðirullin
and she laughed in my face.

How's that for comedy?

Answer 5

We return to what returns. Our ghosts proceed
down streets they lately inhabited.
We meet them in parks and cafes,
in restaurants where we once glimpsed them eating
and where they now look out to see us pass,
recognising something of themselves.

But which of us is which confuses them,
and so they rise, dazzled, from their chairs
and head outside in hope of following us
to a home they might belong to.

Our eyelids burn.
We sense the vertigo they suffer.
We suffer with them. We explode with laughter
Then we wake and rise.

Question 6

Yellow overdue uranium
where evil resides eventually.
Amendments
let everything turn dour or wasteful. Noon.

Are newspapers dead?

I
act, media
actions.
        Coward.

Answer 6

1
The code words in the system
Are pure guesswork. How long do we have?

2
The radioactivity in stones
Can be measured in units of light and ice.

3
The waste remains, the journals rattle on.
The dead are overdue, the cowards.

4
Evil considers its fingernails. It is
Urgently seeking an amendment.

5
Uranium! We have struck gold!
This is the noon we have been waiting for.

ANGELA TOPPING

Question 1

There are lasers on the penon
from where I sit, burnt, burning
through Douglas Adams. Some sort
of sign sought from kids in the pool,
or drunks on the boardwalk. Emerald green
against a brilliant Jade, marking space
between the rocks. And all I can do is hope
the wildcats don't chase lasers like their
domestic counterparts, and reminisce
of my own cats, back at home. Where does
your mind travel to, when you're far from
the comfort of your own bed?

Answer 1

Perhaps I am a bird. Let's say a sparrow.
I dive down a chimney or spurt
through a tall open window
circle round Italian galleries
mistaking the art for real landscapes.

Or perhaps I am a fish. Let's say a carp.
I allow Danube's waters to love through me,
conscious of little but survival.
I flick my tail fin and feel its power,
as I glitter in my chain mail.

I am a bee entering the tunnel of a foxglove,
burrowing into air turned pink and freckled.
I bathe in seas of lavender, my fur sticky
with pollen, prepare for the coming cold,
the winter clustering.

A bird again, this time a swallow
I fly high across continents
guided by magnetism or some other
dark force I have to follow,
my companions around me.

I am higher than tall towers;
deeper than oceans; lost
in the music of the spheres;
rooted in the secrets of the earth.
I am alive, in all my senses.

Question 2

My mind has been occupied with Frank's cousin
and his mermaid. I heard wolves [or Wolves] in
the mix, while I don't claim to see the future I
saw greatness in both record and recorded. If
I could sing, I'd scratch my poems onto the
inside of my lungs, find wings like yours and
bellow from parabronchi. How do you make
your poetry sing? I can't even keep mine in
key.

Answer 2

Rhythm is easy, iambic heartsong
slipsliding of trochees
complicated butter pats of anapests
being slapped into shape by grooved pine boards,
runaway train of dactyls clacking along
Scansion is the salve for grazes

but melody arises pianissimo, tentative
trying to find the right key, the phrase
that opens up the arc and soars
until each crotchet and quaver finds
where it belongs on the stave
and the cadence
moves on in inevitable flow
to a new beginning.

Question 3

I'm clinging onto the belief
that genius comes from working
with all of the lights on. POWER.
Creating a monster needs blood
on the leaves of paper. Do you
build your work on sight? Or
are you bound to other conventions?

Answer 3

I buy the salted popcorn, bring a blanket
settle down in the best seats
to watch the movie with my inner eye.
Not just sight but a feely, smells and taste.
My mind's eye is a quality cinema.

But most often, the poem comes
like a lover, to whisper in my ear
teasing phrases I can barely catch,
then runs away laughing.

I need all my skills to interpret
the other side of my brain, pin down
the wriggling, tantalising words.

Question 4

I found my father fighting the miners
under the streetlights – shaped triangular
– shaped unwanted. He never blew
glass into clouds, toned down the mayhem
of his youth, or resented throwing batteries
at the heads of immigrants. These were
stories of pride, tales of the fights he won
as a small right-wing Acton kid. As if
shanking some kid is a prospective gold
medal
> [I've used this line before] [I've noted my repetition
> before] [What are we if we aren't just the signals of
> our memories?] [Like a broken fucking record] [I've
> used that before too]

Answer 4

A line or phrase from a forgotten draft
can be prized loose and hammered
into a different poem, like a stud
in an old oak door, or a gem
embedded into silver.

It may wander until it finds
a new place to exist, or be lost
like junk in a jumbled drawer.

Memory too. Polish and shine,
add new flourishes, build it up
till it's bright and new.

But beware. Beware of chanting
the same spells too often
else they may lose their magic.

Question 5

We caressed the reservoir's rapids
in the hope they'd cradle us and rear
us instead of our parents,
take us back to the sea
and lay our sinuous milk-laden bodies
on the turf of the tide.
There were giants in the back
of pick-up trucks stealing concrete
from the lids of mine shafts.
We saw our reflections wave back at us
some 70 metres under Mrs Bangka's parking space,
two smiles for every concern.
Are these uncertain forms to be taken seriously?
Do we run when we see
ourselves deeper than the cathedral?
We called the names of our ancestors
and swore we'd burn every bridge we had
if it would clear our names from
the Redruth school register,
if we could just be cradled
and swaddled in tin,
if we could ride the oceans back
to the acorn our universe grew from.

Answer 5

Spooled in my nucleus, the combined threads twisted together
lie the instructions, the form I took, the knots that make me up.
My mum's blue eyes and fine hair, my dad's plump cheeks
and worker's hands, though unlike his, my cuticles are buried.
I went out into the world where they could never venture
to take my present form. They would not know me now.

Poems choose their form. I listen and do not hold them back,
Let them be the things they mean to be, though knarled
And rambling sometimes like old trees, or neat in the small house
Of the sonnet, gathering their blankets round them in rhymes.
There's always my fingerprint, my heartbeat, thrumming
Behind them, though they travel far from me.

KIMMY WALTERS

Question 1

Porquoi Mozart while Morricone conducts
a theatre in paradise? First trimester in A
major, completely static but for orchestral
compositions of Veneta, of fourteen weeks,
fourteen midnights, fourteen full moons.

Keep the unjust heart still, entwine hands
for the final proof of my love. Have you lit
censored film? Alfredo's memories burnt
with The Firemen of Viggiú, fourteen weeks,
fourteen midnights, fourteen full moons.

Elena and Salvatore frozen in love without
the director's revisions. Break F sharp minor
for a nervous D major. Find Palazzo Adriano
in the throws of maternity wards, where
even in winter I'll be the brightest sun.

Answer 1

it's very hard to know anything
about the past and harder still
to encounter any new information about it

we can only puncture the dirt
looking for clues or
try to time travel

but most people fail to consider the linguistic
limitations of time travel

barely anyone can understand you
even when you're not fifty or four hundred
years ago

like right now what do I have?

tiny number of french words
large number of english ones
none in italian
and I can't read music either

if I were somewhere unfamiliar
in space or time
I'd have to draw fourteen lines
to indicate the length of a fortnight

I'd encourage each line to
represent a day somehow

if I can't figure out how
maybe I should stop calling myself a poet

most people fail to consider that
history is made up of millions
of fortnights

one right after the other
it's relentless

babies keep getting born directly
into them

it's a messy business
il n'y a pas d'autre moyen

is that right?

Question 2

I've been told ghosts are cliché –
and I hear them squeaking messages into
steam on the windows.
It's one of those days, Kimmy,
where I brew everybody's coffee – while
watching all those photos
blend into a crema on the surface of my scars.
I want to watch him burn
an arc of disappointment
across the – false smile of my father's fake teeth grin.
How do you leave
notes – Ouija – across
the depth of wasted genetics?
The nuances are in place, an owl in the corner
of a darkened room
and a bluebird in the heart of some junkie poet.
Yes, ghosts are cliché, but
at least mine have
the decency to haunt me in the daylight.

Answer 2

I'm drinking coffee
that someone else made

because I like to be taken care of
for about 20 minutes at a time

and because lately I have struggled to
make anything for myself…
you might know this,
because it's been months…

on the counter are
two ingredients requiring
only heat to become a meal,
but I am lying down

and they will stay ingredients forever

my friend died but she's
far too practical to become
a ghost

which I admire in a certain way

I tried to imagine her as an old woman
her hair was gray
but the roots were dark

and she was smiling down at me
with something that looked like pity

STU WATSON

Question 1

There are two flies
perpendicular to each other
in the crema on this espresso
and each is telling sweet lies
in the form of riddles.

Parallel universe theory
dictates that both flies
are in a different drink
perhaps soup or water
in a different world…

…and perhaps you and I,
Stu, are applying
a different sheen to the surface
of our language
and coating it in Magyar

or German or Arabic.
Am I the result of my language
or vice versa? Are there two
flies, not sailors,
because an English joke demands?

A barista brings a coffee over,
'excuse me, sir, what are these
sailors doing in my drink?'
'Praying for a God
who doesn't exist, or so it seems.'

Answer 1

If one is Descartes' fly,
set down upon a ceiling grid,

and the other is Hugo's
ecstatic memory of God

the each, one can suppose,
would rather not be pinned

whether nailed down fast before the eye
or lifted toward futurity.

But what one knows
of flies of course colludes

and frames the answers we might beg
of them, unspeaking in their flyness,

stayed quietly like a Wittgensteinian lioness
content to be but in the dryness,

content to feel the warmth
off its rubbed together leg.

Question 2

I could pull a cart with balloon strings
attached to three thousand flies,
and live in the back as a static memory
of all of God's failed jokes.

Do you ever feel like your heartbeat
is always the lowest common denominator?
I salt the numbness with the infinite sun
and the cancerous growth on the edge

of my shadow, reading the dreams
of Murakami's broken unicorn skulls.
Every day from July I will fight the robots
who plan to steal my daughter in endless dreams.

I could pull a cart with balloon strings
and a few dozens owls – but what good
would that do to stop me from staring at the ground
from the edge of a Spanish balcony?

Answer 2

As a teenager I used to think
so frequently of crowds of bats
assuming on synchronic wing
that laughing shape, a human face;

but now I think instead to hear
fine rhythms cut in air by wings
and from that score to force a voice
a noiseless signal which will sing

of maudlin things like Henchard there
upon the bridge just looking down
infamy spread across the town
just staring at his reflection when

appears as if on cue an effigy of him—
what I would not give to be
a swarm of bees or locusts then
to witness that strange fictive man

confronted with the image of his sin—
how might hive-minded hearers turn
the moral of his story round
within the natter of their teeming brains?

Question 3

As a teenager I used to think
of how to get home quickest
without being hit by a baseball
bat upisde my head;

but now I think of how
to get home the quickest
so I can see the glow and glory
of my wife and our (her) bump.

Don't worry about the hive, Stu,
worry about the nectar,
the life blood & all that sweet,
disgusting, gross honey.

How did we let ourselves
become so sickly sweet?
How do we draw lines in the mud
with sticks we broke bones on?

My reflection carries weights
and arms itself with shoes
in the fear that my hometown
will cremate me and forget

to tie my laces.

Answer 3

I once imagined that I'd seen
a scaly green reptilian hand
emerge from out the sodden marsh
sunk in beside my family's land

I told a friend that we could catch
this creature and destroy it there
a reverie then gripping me
reality peeling into air

and I can still see his wide eyes
his baffled look of pure belief
and feel the power in my lie
that power granting not relief

but guilt, awareness that a shift
in tone can swing a person so
as to obscure the truth in mists
that veil all that they know

for me this is the honey of the hive
and also still the stick that swings against
the hive and cracks its brittle muddy walls
the lie is lastly bee eyes gasping
as the queen drops down and falls

so something rhizomatic, mixed
I find when what we want is pure
and unadulterated truth;
but I guess we'll take it, why not, sure,
lest we from that pure truth go poor

Question 4

I've seen that reptilian hand dance in the
cold of the shower, when I'm drying myself
and wasting the air with the toxicity of
interruptions. The taps cold and burning,
the reasons to exist still forming in the marsh
at the back of the room. All the walls are just
excuses to leave the city now, Stu, and I don't
know whether to take a train or walk. Both
are great ways to see the countryside, but
it's really a question of quality over quantity.
Have you scaled the garden wall yet? Found your
neighbours hive and stole all their honey?
The sickness of my voice makes me shudder,
especially when I try to record the mess I've
made of everything and realise life is ok.

At best.

Answer 4

Life is at best okay when edged
On either side by what was once
The possible so fast become
The comforting lineaments of doom,
The cracks that rise out of the earth
To shock and stun, allow for us
To witness this apocalypse of fact
Unharnessed and alighting once again—

It's like the difference between a lawyer
And a barrister, we register the present
Through a different lens
On account of our furious knowledge
Of how close so many other worlds were
And are, though may not be as things
Continue to advance, in fact spread out
Break up in coldly distances of time.

It all sinks in across the gap
The train leaps over reaching out
Expanding tracks divert our course
But still we cannot even see
The open road, that lonely tree
There standing in the periphery
Of our so rapid flight for and against
The currents of the denser dreaming force.

COOPER WILHELM

Question 1

The night time but with the moon
as an anchor
plummeting to Earth.
Two sailors and a pack of cigarettes
swigging rum
on the pack of an apostrophe
[read: catastrophe].

A children's birthday party but the balloons
are made of skulls
and all the candy is buried
sixty
seventy
eighty feet below ground.
Blood-covered hands digging for sugar.

A cinema chain but all the chairs are toenails
and the screen
is made of broken dishes.
The projectionist
tries to screen a film –
The Truman Show –
but it's not in the script.

What does your world
look like, Cooper?

Answer 1

A lady bug alights at the top of a femor like a first bud of spring.
No one notices one small bird reassuring another small bird
as they perch above a ship's plump sail.
I feel like I should be human sometimes when all I want
to be is the air passing through my lungs
the way I'll travel through a train station without getting off the train
watching the doors open and close for nothing.
Boys growing up want to be whatever lightless rock
smashed into the earth and made the moon.
They want to be buckets of protein and chum.
They want to sweat like John Cena.
It's easiest crying in the park
because the trees shushing you with their leaves
would be doing that anyway
so you can feel less guilty for having feelings.
I'm back in town if you want to get a drink
or just wave back at me at this gas station
not sure who I could be.

Question 2

I call them ladybirds,
but ladybug is fine,
it's your shit
and you deal with
it however you want.

(but birds eat bugs)

I read about moon
viewing festivals
in Japan, and proceeded
to write terrible poetry
while looking at a cloud-covered
sky. It never rains here,
but it does flood.

If you were to write a poem
about watching the moon,
what would it look like?

My daughter was born two
weeks ago, and now I have less
lunar time than ever before
and I'm kind of grateful
because she has made me
appreciate my sleep.

Answer 2

I worry about people in boats
because I think they'll be like me.
They'll get nervous that there's nothing over the water
to protect them from being seen, they'll reach
out to the moon and its rockwall grip of cloud
to steady themselves and that
's what makes them drown.

But you have to trust people you can't see not to drown.
And trust people to love you forever right
up until they don't.
And trust yourself to survive
days when no one wants you, not even you.

Like how in a specific district called Kamigata
they have complex pails replete with many foods
they take with them to watch new flowers.

And when they're done with flowers

                         they smash the pails. The cloud
              in front of the moon
              is not the moon.
       The cloud is you

because you see from where no one
else could be at this exact moment.

You are the pail, and you are the watcher of new flowers,
and you are the flowers every second
falling out of bloom.

And we can all be the way people talk about the moon
when they miss someone: same moon millions of miles away
from each other

or

how each moon swells big with the next moon
which looks just like it
and will share the earth
with even more people
and turn their eyes into little moons
and make them beautiful.

Question 3

I invented a language
and made three words
to signify a boat:

Övvurbåt – when a boat is on top of the water
Ündderbåt – when a boat is below the water
Båt – when a boat is not on water.

But really, Cooper, what is a boat
when it isn't on water?
Surely it isn't still a boat?

It's not a wreck either,
because that is ündderbåt
[and so are submarines

                              which basically are floating,
                              shipwrecks as a form of
                              transport and nuclear

destruction]. I guess it is still a vessel
like my body will still have blood vessels
when I've dried up. And neither boat

nor blood will serve it's purpose.

Answer 3

I think of boats as the hardened gelatin
that makes pills from piles
and makes sure sailors aren't dissolved
until they've gotten where they're going safe.

Do you know those pill capsules
are made from what rises to the surface of the water
in which you boil bones?
It's like if your coffin were an exoskeleton
protecting you from the earth until

it sent tendrils through the rot
and your body made it well again.

Though thinking this makes me wonder if the purpose of
blood
and bodies and talking to your friends
were not a kind of drug thing:
the earth deprives its body of ourselves
so it can get first tension then release.

And you are an individual, with your own name to put on a
ticket
to sit forever on a manifest (which I assume ships have
so that there is a sense of revelation
when the dead will all rise saved)

and when you board your coffin
and those who love you send it on its way,
it looks like sinking
but is really just a body
letting in a pill, a mouth swallowing the specific
word it made.

PHILLIP B. WILLIAMS

Question 1

When I write of my mother or father,
I use the word djöfaðirullin because
I constructed it from Demon, and they
built me from their devils. But I worry
it's also because I haven't got the
strength to put them on the lines, and
let them feel the ache of my collapsing
ventricles bleed blue into their realities.
I see them at night, in the corner of my
room counting their eggs before they
smash the shells with their hammered
fists. I still crawl back to memories of
my djöfaðirullin burning the embers
of my dreams at edge of the
sjóndeildarhnífuringur – horizon on a
knife's edge – and hear them spit
shrapnel into the collar of my school
shirts. I still can't bring myself to hurt
them in words without that layer of
protection. Do you cover your tracks,
Phillip? Do you coat the past in thick
tar and hope you can murder your
djöfaðirullin without having to twist the knife?

Answer 1
[PETRICHOR]

Isn't the maggot the oldest form
of faith? How even Jesus could
not command it stop its cleansing
His wounds, so devoted? Didn't
the flesh that was soft, had failed even Him,
fall softer into what would be
dust? And now my father's grave.

My shadow across it performs love

which is nothing more than lying down
while a hard rain disarms the trees
of their autumnal leaves, blows around
the veined fire until one lands
on his headstone, a lamp. Yes,
I see him more clearly now,
as though for the first time.

MARK YAKICH

Question 1

My epaulets were branded game,
held aloft in the corridors beside
nuclear deterrents. Carved bâton
percé into my ironed creases and
the blood on the inside of my lip.
Do you bite through your memories?
Chew the vestibule in nervous wait?
Anteocularis fell before my eyes
as I was reminded of the first note.

Answer 1

Falling through the skylights,
Your triolets wouldn't open properly,
Unkempt yet unmitigated. Did I ever
Go pulse-less in your mind? End
The alley of happiness on purpose?
Too light already to go faded.
Much too forgetful to write good prose.

Question 2

Do you ever find yourself
  floating
    unaided
      held together by repetition?

I repeat all of my weaknesses,
  lock my traumas away
    with the phrases
      I keep echoing in my work.

Answer 2

I'd rather lose than win
And have to empathize
With the one who lost.

Question 3

On Pika
            (From Hiroshima – meaning
                                brilliant light,
                    meaning the moment
                                I beg to be able
                    to tell somebody about)

Trapp
            (From Norwegian – meaning
                                staircase,
                    meaning the location
                                I find myself
                    begging to forget about)

I was warned that silence
would be essential
if we wanted to maintain the
family unit.

And to this day I still keep quiet
through fear
of destroying a cult
I no longer belong to.
            Do you write the words you
                                were told
                    to never say, or do
                                you cover them
                    in metaphor?)

Answer 3
[Mum and Dad]
          for Philip Larkin

they
  were

  so
alike

  that
  to

tell
  each

  other
apart

  they
  called

each
  other

  unspeakable
names

Question 4

Today
            .nobody showed up
            to hear me tell them
I stole my script back,
tore the print from
the inside of a scope
            I never believed in.
And for some reason
            I expected these

                    g
                            h
            o
            s
            t
                    s

to believe in me.
But how can you help
            when nobody cares enough
            o melt into your words?

Answer 4

Even if I don't like somebody, I think that somebody must like him or her so I try harder, but sometimes I think that if somebody else likes that person then I don't have to.
I live on a one-way street.

*

I am an average chess player.
I prefer to hide than to seek.

*

I do not write books.
I dig holes and then, forgetting that I've made them, I fall.

*

Our son collects pebbles every chance he gets and cares for them as though they were pet bugs, but then when he finds bugs he mostly wants to chuck them as though they were pebbles.
I find golf a good way to ruin a long walk.

*

One Christmas Day, I challenged my dad to a game of chess and beat him, only later realizing that my winning was a terrible mistake.
I don't know whether it's better to cry in car parks than to hand feed the elderly.

*

I often feel closer to the things that humans make than to the humans who make them.
The diaries I have kept in my life are all stored in a plastic box with a flimsy lock.

LAY OUT YOUR UNREST

Printed in Poland
by Amazon Fulfillment
Poland Sp. z o.o., Wrocław